# If Thou Wilt Be Perfect . . .

## Talks on Spiritual Philosophy

### Oswald Chambers

SIMPKIN, MARSHALL, HAMILTON, KENT & CO., LTD.
LONDON

CROSSREACH
PUBLICATIONS

*HOPE. INSPIRATION. TRUST.*

# CONTENTS

Introduction ......................................................................4

I. The Philosophy of Perfection ...................................7
II. The Philosophy of the Fall—I ...............................18
III. The Philosophy of the Fall—II .............................25
IV. The Philosophy of Discernment ...........................32
V. The Philosophy of Following Our Lord.................40
VI. The Philosophy of Godliness.................................48
VII. The Philosophy of Reason....................................56
VIII. The Philosophy of Love .....................................65
IX. The Philosophy of Sacrificing...............................74
X. The Philosophy of Discipleship ..............................81
XI. The Philosophy of the Perfect Life........................88
XII. The Disciple and the Lord of Destiny .................94

About CrossReach Publications ...................................99
Bestselling Titles from CrossReach.............................. 100

# INTRODUCTION

## *If Thou Wilt Be Perfect*

## Source

Lectures on biblical philosophy given at the Bible Training College, London, from January to July 1912.

## Publication History

- As articles: First published as articles in the *Bible Training Course (BTC) Monthly Journal* from October 1937 through October 1938.

- As a book: First published as a book in 1939. Mrs. Chambers had planned to title it *Spiritual Philosophy* but bowed to David Lambert's suggestion to use Jesus' words to the rich young ruler in Matthew 19:21—"If thou wilt be perfect."

Always a voracious reader of wide-ranging taste, Chambers included the writings of many philosophers in his personal study. During Oswald's student days at the University of Edinburgh (1895-1896), he very likely studied Metaphysics and the History of Philosophy under Professor Andrew Seth and Moral Philosophy under Professor Henry Calderwood. In addition, he may well have attended Dr. Alexander Whyte's Young Men's Classes, held every Sunday evening following the service at Free St. George's Church. When Chambers arrived in Edinburgh, Dr. Whyte was dealing with "The Mystics," including Tauler and the book, *Theologia Germanica,* which are both quoted throughout *If Thou Wilt Be Perfect.*

In 1900, Chambers was teaching philosophy at Dunoon College, a small theological school across the Firth of Clyde from Glasgow, Scotland. When his students, most of whom had no university training, expressed their difficulty in making sense of existing textbooks, Chambers compiled and published his own *Outlines for the Study of Historical Philosophy* as a guide for his classes.

Of his lecture series on Biblical Philosophy at the Bible Training College in 1912, Chambers said: "The Ethics and Philosophy classes have taken a great stride in advance, and this is all the more surprising as the Bible Philosophy class is anything but a popular subject as commonly conceived; yet the numbers attending this class grow."

One of Chambers' recurring themes was the critical necessity for every Christian to think. "The reason why the average Christian worker is only the average Christian worker," Oswald told his students, "is that he or she will remain grossly ignorant about what he does not see any need for. All of you have intelligence, and you must use it for God."

### Foreword

## On Tauler and on *Theologia Germanica*

Two names are mentioned in this book, one is a man, Tauler, and the other a volume, *Theologia Germanica.* Quotations are made from them. Both belong to pre-Reformation times. John Tauler was born in Strasbourg about 1300. He was a Dominican monk and had already achieved honour and reputation as a preacher when a great change occurred in his spiritual outlook. An unknown layman, after hearing him preach, was moved to tell him that he was allowing himself to be "killed by the letter," and was yet in darkness, and had not tasted the sweetness of the Holy Ghost. The preacher took the words in a spirit of meekness and was ready to receive helpful counsel from his unknown friend. "You must," he said, "take up your cross and follow our Lord Jesus Christ and His example in utter sincerity, humility and patience, and must let go all your proud reasoning." He advised him to cease his preaching for a while and in quiet contemplation examine his life in the mirror of our Lord's. Tauler was nearly fifty, but he took the place of abasement and self-surrender, and for nearly two years was a seeker of God's way, praying that God's life might be brought forth in him. His former friends thought him demented. When the clear light came and he knew the time had come to bear his witness in public, he found it not easy to begin, but soon wisdom and grace from the Holy Spirit were bestowed in abundant measure. So began years of wonderful work for God. In those days when salvation by simple faith in Jesus Christ was so largely hidden beneath ceremonial worship, he taught many that the way to God was by a New Birth that brought men into a vital relation to the *Living God.* His sermons greatly influenced Luther. They have ministered to many in many countries. A volume of his sermons has been published in English under the title, *The Following of Christ.*

The book, *Theologia Germanica,* belongs to the same period. Its author is unknown. That also prepared for the Reformation, as it lays stress on the Holy Spirit's application of Christ's work to the heart of a believer. God never leaves Himself without a witness, and in that bedimmed period these lights were shining and have been shining ever since.

John Wesley complained to William Law that when he was an earnest inquirer he had been directed to the mystic writers, and so had missed the basic truth of salvation by faith in Jesus Christ. We all need to know the initial experience of Christ as the Propitiation for our sins, and as the One who has brought to a world of sinners the abundance of grace and the *gift* of righteousness. Afterwards we may find, as Wesley did, much light in such writers as the above upon how God works in us to will and to do of His good pleasure, and how we can work out our own salvation (Philippians 2:12-13).

The quotations made by Oswald Chambers are themselves of great value, and the expository words that follow are full of luminous and practical teaching for us to-day.

London
David Lambert
April 1939

# I. The Philosophy of Perfection

*But when that which is perfect is come, that which is in part shall be done away. 1 Corinthians 13:10 (RV)*

*"That which is perfect" is a Being, who hath comprehended and included all things in Himself and His own Substance, and without whom, and besides whom, there is no true Substance, and in whom all things have their Substance.*

## That Which Is Perfect

The Bible reveals that "that which is perfect" is a Being. God is the only Perfect Being; no human being is perfect apart from God. We make the blunder of applying to human beings terms which the Bible applies to God only. Our Lord in replying to the rich young ruler, who used the term "Good Master," said, "None is good save One, even God" (RV). There is only one Being to whom the term "good" can be applied, and that is the Perfect Being, the term cannot be applied to good men. In the Sermon on the Mount our Lord places God as the model for Christian character; He does not say, "Be good as a man is good," but—"Ye therefore shall be perfect, as your heavenly Father is perfect" (RV). We are to be perfect as our Father in heaven is perfect, not by struggle and effort, but by the impartation of that which is Perfect. We are accustomed to the use of the word "perfect" in connection with our relationship to God (e.g. Philippians 3:12-15), but here the word is used in a bigger sense, viz. perfect as God is perfect.

"Love" is another term we are apt to apply wrongly. We emphasise perfect love towards our fellow-men; the Bible emphasises perfect love to God. Love is an indefinable word, and in the Bible it is always used as directly characteristic of God— "God is love." In Romans 5:5, Paul says that "the love of God is shed abroad in our hearts," not the power to love God, but the love of God.

Or take Truth. The Truth is our Lord Himself, consequently any part of the truth may be a lie unless it leads to a relation to *the*

Truth. Salvation, sanctification, the Second Coming are all parts of the Truth, but none is the Truth; and they are only parts of the Truth as they are absorbed by the Truth, our Lord Himself. We are not told to expound the way of salvation, or to teach sanctification, but to lift up Jesus, i.e. to proclaim the truth.

## That Which Is in Part

> *If any man thinketh that he knoweth anything, he knoweth not yet as he ought to know. (1 Corinthians 8:2 RV)*

God wants us to lose our definitions and become rightly related to Himself, the Perfect One. If we try and state before God where we are in experience, we find we cannot do it, though we know with a knowledge "which passeth knowledge." The purpose of God is to get the part into the whole; if we remain in the part by sticking to our convictions, to that which we know, we shall fizzle off. An experience that is true and vivid cannot be stated in words, the lines of definition are gone. Our experience is only part of the Perfect. Jesus Christ is much more than we have experienced Him to be.

> *But "that which is in part," or the imperfect, is that which hath its source in, or springeth from the Perfect, just as a brightness or a visible appearance floweth out from the sun or a candle, and appeareth to be somewhat, this or that. And it is called a creature, and of all these "things which are in part," none is the Perfect.*

Are we resting in our experience of the Truth, or in the Truth? The part has its source in the Perfect. The experiences of salvation and sanctification spring from the perfect Source, and it is this that gives the devil his chance to come as an angel of light and make us seek experiences instead of Christ. Do we lift up Jesus, or are we busy carefully defining our religious experiences, having this measuring-rod for the Almighty and that measuring-rod for the saints, which if they do not come up to we say they are wrong? There is always a danger of doing this so long as we walk by convictions. If our experiences come from the true Source and are untouched, they will lead to one place only—to the fulness of the life of God; but if they are tampered with they will lead away from God. Satan does not tempt saints to tell lies or to steal or drink, he does not come to them in that way; he comes along the line of their experiences, he seeks to separate Christian experience from the Lord Jesus and make us want to hug a certain type of experience for ourselves.

When we have part of the Perfect nature in us and are walking in the light of the Holy Spirit, He will take us surely and certainly to the Source from which the experience sprang, viz. God—unless we prefer to stay in our experience. Are we living in the light of our convictions, prescribed and confined, or are we living the life hid with Christ in God?

To those who have had no spiritual experience it sounds absurd to talk about being one with God in Christ, absurd to talk about being guided by the Spirit, they are impatient with it; of course they are, they must be made part of the Perfect (i.e. be born from above, RV MG) before they can understand the language of the Perfect in experience.

Jesus Christ must always be much more than any Christian experience. This throws a flood of light on experiences. That which is Perfect is God, that which is part is the creature experience. The creature experience has its source in God, but if looked at in itself it is apart altogether from God; when looked at in God it takes us straight to God Himself. When God ceases a way of guiding, when He removes the symbols of His presence, when answers to prayer do not come, it is because He is bringing us to the place where the part is merged in the Perfect, and we in our degree are becoming what Jesus wants us to be.

There is only one way to understand the Perfect and the part in relation to it, and that is by receiving the Holy Spirit; God will give us the Holy Spirit if we ask Him (Luke 11:13). We need to receive the Holy Spirit, not only for Christian experience but to bring us into perfect union with God.

## That Which Is Perception (1 Corinthians 2:11-16; 1 John 2:27)

Perception means the power of discernment. "To whom hath the arm of the Lord been revealed?" (RV). We all see the common occurrences of daily life, but who amongst us can perceive the arm of the Lord behind them? who can perceive behind the thunder the voice of God? The characteristic of the man without the Spirit of God is that he has no power of perception, he cannot perceive God's working behind ordinary occurrences. The events of ordinary days and nights present facts we cannot explain, the only way to explain them is by receiving the Spirit of God Who will impart to us an interpretation that will keep the heart strong and confident in God, because it gives us an understanding of God Who is behind all things; but to the one who is not there, the explanations seem absurd.

Perception in the natural world is called intuition—I know I know, although I do not know how I know. In the spiritual world this knowledge is the "anointing" the Apostle John alludes to. When the Holy Spirit is in us He will never let us stop at the part experience. He will cause our part experience to keep us always one with the Perfect and will reveal God to us. If ever we imagine that the Spirit of God gives us an illumination apart from the written Word, Satan is twisting the truth, and it is this kind of passage that he distorts most.

> The things which are in part cannot be apprehended, known and expressed; but the Perfect cannot be apprehended, known and expressed by any creature as creature.

Peter tells us to be ready always to give an answer to every man that asketh you a reason concerning the hope that is in us. He did not say give reasonings, but a reason. We can give a reason for that we know, but we cannot reason it out with the man who has not the same spirit. We can state that we are right with God because we have received His Spirit on the word of Jesus, but our reasonings are nonsense to the man who has not accepted the Holy Spirit.

## The Coming of the Perfect (John 17:22; Psalm 86:11)

> *Now when that which is Perfect is come, then that which is*
> *in part shall be done away. But when doth it come? I say, when*
> *as much as may be, it is known, felt and tasted of the soul...*
> *So also God who is the Highest Good, willeth not to hide*
> *Himself from any, wheresoever He findeth a devout soul, that*
> *is thoroughly purified from all creatures. For in what measure*
> *we put off the creature, in the same measure are we able to put*
> *on the Creator, neither more nor less.*

"That they may be one"—in experience? No, "that they may be one, even as We are one." That is infinitely beyond experience, it is a perfect oneness not only in adjustment but in realisation. In our spiritual experience it means knowing that—"In all the world there is none but Thee, my God, there is none but Thee." Other people have become shadows, the creature we used to rely upon has proved a broken reed, the spiritual experience we built upon has deserted us, the methods of guidance that used to bless our souls starve us now. This is illustrated in the purifying of Abraham's faith, the purification went on until Abraham was lost in God. He did not lose his identity, he reached his identity in God. The hymns that are full of absorption in God are true of deepest spiritual experience, but only true in the fundamental sense, in the surface sense they are in error.

The Psalmist prayed, "Unite my heart to fear Thy name"—the whole spirit, soul and body so united with God that the soul does not think separately of body, soul or spirit, but only of God. There are false unities possible in a man's experience whereby man's spirit, soul and body are brought into harmony. Paul calls these things idolatry, because idolatry is the uniting of body, soul and spirit to the wrong god.

If we are despising the chastening of the Lord and fainting when rebuked of Him, it is because we do not understand what God is doing; He is weaning us from creatures to Himself, from the things we have been united to instead of being united to Him only. When God is weaning a soul from creatures, from Christian experience, from teachers and friends, then is the time that the devil begins the advocacy of self-pity. Satan tried to make Jesus realise Himself apart from God (see Matthew 16:23), but He would not—"For I am come down from heaven, not to do Mine own will, but the will of Him that sent Me" (RV). When we are filled with the Holy Spirit He unites us body, soul and spirit with God until we are one with God even as Jesus was. This is the meaning of the Atonement—at-one-ment with God.

The one perfect Personality is our Lord. When we separate ourselves from Jesus we are in part, we are not perfect but when the life of Jesus comes into us we no more think of the separating of spirit, soul and body, we think of Jesus only. Remember, we are not sanctified for our sakes, but for God's sake. How many of us are trying to exploit God with the diplomacy which the world uses? We try to exploit God when we pray—"O Lord, give me this gift, this experience." That is the spirit which springs from the devil, we are trying to ape being devout souls, trying to be like Christians, but wanting a relation to God on our own lines. We can only get rightly related to God through Jesus Christ. The coming of the Perfect means that we are made one with God by Jesus. Immediately we are rightly related to God, perfectly adjusted to Him, the Perfect life comes to us and through us.

## The Conversion of the Part

> . . . it is impossible to the creature in virtue of its creature-nature and qualities, that of which it saith "I" and "myself" to be perfect. For in whatsoever creature the Perfect shall be known, therein the creature-nature and qualities, I, the Self and the like, must all be lost and done away.

Our Lord told the rich young ruler to fling away all he had, to think of himself as possessing nothing—"Be a mere conscious man and give that manhood to Me. Lose altogether the sense of yourself as one who wants to be blessed and be related to God in Me" (see Matthew 19:21).

*So long as we think much of these things, cleave to them with love, joy, pleasure or desire, so long remaineth the Perfect unknown to us.*

If we seek the baptism of the Holy Ghost in order that God may make us great servants of His, we shall never receive anything. God baptises us with the Holy Ghost that He may be All in all.

Numbers of people say, "I have asked God to sanctify me and He has not done it." Of course He has not! Do we find one word in the Bible which tells us to pray, "Lord, sanctify me"? What we do read is that God sanctifies what we give. An unconditional "give up" is the condition of sanctification, not claiming something for ourselves. This is where unscriptural holiness teaching has played so much havoc with spiritual experience. We receive from God on one condition only, viz. that we yield ourselves to Him and are willing to receive nothing. Immediately we state conditions and say, "I want to be filled with the Holy Spirit," "I want to be delivered from sin," "I want to be the means of saving souls"—we may pray to further orders, but an answer will never come that way. That is all the energy of the flesh, it has no thought of the claims of Jesus on the life. Are we willing to be baptised into His death? How much struggle is there in a dead man? How much assertion of "I" and "me" and "mine"—"I have had such a wonderful experience"? The Spirit of God will never witness to testimonies along that line, they are not true to the genius of the Holy Ghost, not true to the nature of Jesus. "Whosoever shall confess Me before men," said Jesus. If there is a tightness and a dryness in our experience it is because we have begun to take the advice of someone other than God, have begun to try and make our experience like someone else said it should be. "But they, . . . measuring themselves by themselves, and comparing themselves with themselves, are without understanding" (RV).

## The Concentration of Perception (John 15:5; Philippians 4:13)

*That which hath flowed forth from it, is no true Substance, and hath no Substance except in the Perfect, but is an accident, or a brightness, or a visible appearance, which is no Substance, and hath no Substance except in the fire whence the brightness flowed forth, such as the sun or a candle.*

"Without Me ye can do nothing." If we are not spiritual we will say that is not true, but if we are spiritual we know it is true. Our Lord said many things that are only true in the domain in which He spoke them. For instance, He said, "Ye have not life in yourselves" (John 6:53 RV). We have life, but not in the domain Jesus means. We are alive physically, alive morally and intellectually without Jesus, but we are not alive spiritually. "Ye have not *this* life in yourselves." "If any man willeth to do His will, he shall know of the teaching, whether it be of God, or whether I speak from Myself" (RV). What is God's will? That we should receive His Spirit, and God will give us the Holy Spirit if we ask. If we put ourselves in the condition of paupers and waive all right to the gift and are willing to receive, then Jesus said, God will put into us the Spirit that is in Him. When we have received the Holy Spirit we begin to realise that what Jesus said is true, "without Me ye can do nothing"—in the spiritual life. If some of us are asked to give our testimony, to speak in the open air, to take a meeting, we faint because we have not learned the lesson of drawing on the Perfect life, of drawing on Jesus. "Without Me"—nothing; but—"I can do all things through Christ which strengtheneth me."

Have we ever come to the place of saying, "Lord, do in me all Thou dost want to do?" We ask God to do much less than this and think we are asking for tremendous things; we have to come to the place of saying, "Lord, I ask that Thy will may be done in me." The will of God is the gladdest, brightest, most bountiful thing possible to conceive, and yet some of us talk of the will of God with a terrific sigh—"Oh well, I suppose it is the will of God," as if His will were the most calamitous thing that could befall us.

Are we learning to think and perceive and interpret Christian experience along this line? When people come to us, are we so relying on the Holy Spirit that He can easily lead them to Jesus, or are we trying to make their square lives fit into our round experience, trying to fit their broad experience into our poor narrow waistcoat-pocket experience? We are off our territory on those lines; we are here for one purpose only, to be taken up with Jesus.

## The Principle of Sin (1 John 5:8-12)

> *The Scripture and the Faith and the Truth say, Sin is nought else, but that the creature turneth away from the unchangeable Good and betaketh itself to the changeable; that is to say, that it turneth away from the Perfect to "that which is in part" and imperfect, and most often to itself.*

This is the principle of sin. Anything in spiritual life or in sensual life that makes us draw our life from anything less than God is of the essence of sin. God made man to have dominion over the life of the sea and air and earth, but God was to have dominion over man. Adam sinned by taking his claim to his right to himself. This claim to my right to myself works in those who are born again, and it is called "the carnal mind." It expresses itself like this—"I want the baptism of the Holy Ghost; I want to be sanctified; I want to be filled with the Spirit; I want to be used of God." All that springs from the wrong source, it is not drawing its life from the right place. When we receive and recognise and rely on the Holy Spirit, all that stops for ever. We have to "walk in the light, as He is in the light," the light that Jesus walked in (see John 6:38; 14:10).

## The Presence of Sin (John 5:30-32; Romans 1:25)

> *When the creature claimeth for its own anything good, such as Substance, Life, Knowledge, Power, and in short whatever we should call good, as if it were that, or possessed that, or that were itself or that proceeded from it—as often as this cometh to pass, the creature goeth astray.*

The one characteristic of love is that it thinks of nothing for itself, it is absorbed in God. "Love suffereth long, and is kind; love envieth not . . . love taketh not account of the evil." We cannot live as Jesus lived by trying to imitate Him. "Jesus called a little child to Him, and set him in the midst of them, and said, Except ye . . . become as little children, ye shall in no wise enter into the kingdom of heaven." Our Lord was not setting up a child as an ideal, but as a fact. A child does not work from a conscious ambition, it obeys the law of the life that is in him without thinking. When we are born again and rightly related to God we will live the right kind of life without thinking. Immediately we begin to think about it, we fix our eyes on our own whiteness and go wrong. Much of the holiness teaching of to-day makes people fix their eyes on their own whiteness, not on Jesus Christ—"I give up this and that, I fast here, I do this and the other, I will give up anything and everything to possess a perfect life." We will never get it in that way, but only by the passion of an absolute devotion to Jesus and that is only possible by receiving the Holy Spirit and obeying Him.

## The Propagation of Sin (1 John 3:4-8; Isaiah 14:12-13; 2 Thessalonians 2:4; Colossians 2:20-23)

> *What did the devil do else, or what was his going astray and his fall else, but that he claimed for himself to be also somewhat, and would have it that somewhat was his, and something was due to him? This setting up of a claim and his "I" and "me" and "mine," these were his going astray, and his fall. And thus it is to this day.*

John's argument is not to do with an act of sin, but with the disposition of sin. It is this that the devil propagates in human beings. Why don't we realise what God's Book says? We talk about chopping off this, and doing that, and having times of consecration to God. The only test of holiness is that the life of Jesus is being manifested in our mortal flesh, and that we are not appealed to on the lines He was not appealed to on; nothing springs up in us and says, "Now that is mine." The perfect love is given to us freely by the grace of God, and we can hinder it when we like, no matter what our experience has been, if we cease drawing on the life of God. Anything we possess as our own, as a possession of our own personality, is the very essence and principle of sin at work. "If any man will come after Me," said Jesus, "let him deny himself"; literally, let him give up his right to himself to Me, "and take up his cross daily, and follow Me." Our Lord said this over and over again, but we have come to the conclusion that He did not mean what He said and we piously and reverently pass it over.

*The quotations are from the book entitled Theologia Germanica.*

# II. THE PHILOSOPHY OF THE FALL—I

## Boundless Inheritance of Covetousness

> *What shall we say then? Is the law sin? God forbid.*
> *Nay, I had not known sin, but by the law: for I had*
> *not known lust, except the law had said, Thou shalt*
> *not covet. (Romans 7:7)*

> *It is said, it was because Adam ate the apple that he was lost,*
> *or fell. I say, it was because of his claiming something for his*
> *own, and because of his I, Mine, Me and the like. Had he*
> *eaten seven apples, and yet never claimed anything for his*
> *own, he would not have fallen: but as soon as he called*
> *something his own, he fell, and would have fallen if he had*
> *never touched an apple.*

What is true of Adam is true of every man and woman, and "not all mankind could amend his fall, or bring him back from going astray." This inheritance of covetousness is the very essence of the Fall, and no praying and no power of man, singly or banded together, can ever avail to touch it; the only thing that can touch it is the great Atonement of our Lord Jesus Christ. Lust and covetousness are summed up in the phrase, "I must have it at once and for myself." It is an absolute flood in the nature of man, it overtakes his spirit, it overtakes his soul and body. In some natures the spirit of covetousness works through the body and is seen in sordid ways; sometimes it is kept back and only in man's reason is it manifested; and sometimes it is held still further back and suppressed, but it is there. The background of the whole thing is the lust of possessing according to my affinities.

## (a) Birth of Death

"*For in the day that thou eatest thereof thou shalt surely die*" (Genesis 2:17). Death is the inheritance of the whole human race; since Adam, no man has ever been alive to God saving by the supernatural act of re-birth. Do not get the idea that because man did not die suddenly physically, he is not dead. The manifestation of death in the body is simply a matter of time, "For in the day that thou eatest thereof thou shalt surely die." The birth of death was in that moment; not the birth of death for one man, but the birth of the death of the whole human race. God's attitude revealed in the Bible towards men is that they are "dead in trespasses and sins"; no touch with God, not alive towards God at all, they are quite indifferent to God's claims.

### (b) The Bye-Law of Death

"*For if by one man's offence death reigned by one . . .*" (Romans 5:17). A bye-law is a supplementary regulation, and the bye-law of death is a supplementary regulation on account of disobedience. "For I was alive without the law once," said the Apostle Paul, "but when the commandment came, sin revived, and I died. And the commandment, which was ordained to life, I found to be unto death" (Romans 7:9-10). We are all alive apart from God in our own consciousness, and when preachers talk about being dead in trespasses and sins, good worldly-minded men and women are amused at our being so stupid as to tell them they are dead. They say, "I am alive, my body is alive; my mind and heart and soul and spirit are alive; what do you mean by being dead?" But immediately a soul comes into contact with Jesus Christ's standard, instantly the realisation comes of what death means.

### (c) Branded by Death

"*For the wages of sin is death*" (Romans 6:23). Every natural virtue is death-branded, because the natural virtues are remnants of a ruined humanity, they are not promises of an evolving perfection. Take the life of the intellect or of the spirit, where does it end? "He that increaseth knowledge increaseth sorrow." Love produces such pain (apart from a knowledge of God) that it makes the sensitive soul wonder if it is worth while to love. Death is everywhere, on the attainments of the mind, of the heart and spirit. When you try to approach God in prayer and draw near to Him, you find the curse of this disposition of covetousness—"I must have this for myself, I want to be right with God for my own sake"—and it saps the energy out of devotion, out of communion with God and Christian service, until the soul is almost wrung to despair. It is that kind of thing which made the Apostle Paul say—"sold under sin."

We have to get down to this aspect of sin which is not familiar to us as a rule.

Talk about conviction of sin! I wonder how many of us have ever had one five minutes' conviction of sin. It is the rarest thing to know of a man or woman who has been convicted of sin. I am not sure but that if in a meeting one or two people came under the tremendous conviction of the Holy Ghost, the majority of us would not advocate they should be put in a lunatic asylum, instead of referring them to the Cross of Christ. We are unfamiliar nowadays with this tremendous conviction of sin, which Paul refers to as being "sold under sin," but it is not a bit too strong to say that when once the Spirit of God convicts a man of sin, it is either suicide or the Cross of Christ, no man can stand such conviction long. We have any amount of conviction about pride and wrong dealing with one another, but when the Holy Ghost convicts He does not bother us on that line, He gives us the deep conviction that we are living in independence of God, of a death away from God, and we find all our virtues and goodness and religion has been based on a ruinous thing, viz. the boundless inheritance of covetousness. That is what the Fall means. Let it soak into your thinking, and you will understand the marvel of the salvation of Jesus Christ which means deliverance from covetousness, root and branch. Never lay the flattering unction to your soul that because you are not covetous for money or worldly possessions, you are not covetous for anything. The fuss and distress of owning anything is the last remnant of the disposition of sin. Jesus Christ possessed nothing for Himself (see 2 Corinthians 8:9). Right through the warp and woof of human nature is the ruin caused by the disposition of covetousness which entered into the human race through the Fall, and it is this disposition which the Holy Spirit convicts of.

### Beatific Incarnation (Romans 5:1-11)

*But how shall my fall be amended? It must be healed as Adam's fall was healed, and on the self-same wise. . . . And in this bringing back and healing, I can, or may, or shall do*

*nothing of myself, but just simply yield to God, so that He
alone may do all things in me and work, and I may suffer Him
and all His work and His divine will.*

The Atonement means that in the Cross of Jesus Christ God
redeemed the whole human race from the possibility of damnation
through the heredity of sin. Jesus Christ never applied the words
"children of the devil" to ordinary sinners, He applied them to
religious disbelievers. Nowhere is it taught in the Bible that we are
by nature children of the devil; Paul says we "were by nature the
children of wrath." How many men and women do we know who
have seen what Jesus Christ came to do, who really knew He came
to save them from sin and who have deliberately said, "No, I won't
let Him"? The majority of men are sheep, as Jesus said, and the bias
of the Fall leads them astray.

### (a) Ruined Race

*"And I will put enmity between thee and the woman, and
between thy seed and her seed; it shall bruise thy head, and thou
shalt bruise his heel"* (Genesis 3:15). The prophecy here does not
refer to the destruction of sin in the individual, but to the
destruction of what the Apostle Paul calls "the body of sin,"
symbolised in the first incarnation of the devil as a serpent. The
body of sin stands as the counterpart of the Mystical Body of
Christ. The fountain head of the body of sin is the devil; the
Fountain Head of the mystical body of Christ is God. The
disposition of covetousness which entered in at the Fall, connects
me with the body of sin; in the personal experience of sanctification
this disposition of covetousness is identified with the Cross of
Christ "that the body of sin might be destroyed." The more people
there are who enter into sanctification through Jesus Christ, the
more is Satan's dominance ruined. The body of sin is maimed and
paralysed by every being who enters into the Mystical Body of
Christ through His salvation. "The carnal mind," which is "enmity
against God," is my connection with the body of sin; but the body
of sin is something infinitely greater than the carnal mind, it is the
mystical body of sin with the devil at its head, which Jesus Christ

came to destroy (1 John 3:8), and in His sanctified children is manifested the bruising of Satan and the enfeebling of the body of sin, until at the final wind-up of everything, the body of sin and the devil are absolutely removed, not only in the individual saints but from the presence of the saints. Satan is not removed now from the presence of the saints, but the saint is still kept in the world where the evil one rules, consequently the saint is continually being badgered by the evil one. Jesus prayed, not that we should be taken out of the world, but that we should be "kept from the evil one" (RV)

### (b) Realised Right of Saved Souls (Romans 6:12-14)

"*Let not sin therefore reign in your mortal body, that ye should obey it in the lusts thereof*" *(*Romans 6:12). Paul is strong in urging us to realise what salvation means in our bodily lives; it means that we command our bodies to obey the new disposition. That is where you find the problems on the margins of the sanctified life. Paul argues in Romans 6:19, "You are perfectly adjusted to God on the inside by a perfect Saviour, but your members have been used as servants of the wrong disposition; now begin to make those same members obey the new disposition." As we go on, we find every place God brings us into is the means of enabling us to realise with growing joy that the life of Christ within is more than a match not only for the enemy on the outside but for the impaired body that comes between. Paul urges with passionate pleading, that we present our bodies a living sacrifice, and then realise, not presumptuously, but with slow, sure, overwhelming certainty that every command of Christ can be obeyed in our bodily life through the Atonement.

### (c) Restricting Remains of Sin

"*What then? Shall we sin, because we are not under the law, but under grace? God forbid. Know ye not, that to whom ye yield yourselves servants to obey, his servants ye are to whom ye obey; whether of sin unto death, or of obedience unto righteousness?*" *(*Romans 6:15-16). A partial realisation on the part of a child of God of the salvation of Jesus Christ is the very thing Satan delights in, because it leaves within that one the remains of the sinful disposition. In regeneration a twofold experience ought to be ours: the introduction into a new kingdom by the incoming of the Holy Spirit and the realisation of forgiveness of sins; and then being borne on to a moral identification with the death of Jesus whereby we know that "our old man is crucified with Him." Impaired lives, impaired judgments and experiences—all that makes us limp and compromising, comes about because we have realised only partially what Jesus Christ came to do, and the great rouser up out of that sleep of indifference is the Apostle Paul. Read his Epistles, rely on the Spirit of God, and let Him drive home these truths to you.

## Freedom for God

> *I am the Lord: that is My name: and My glory will I not give to another. (Isaiah 42:8)*

> *If I call any good thing my own, as if I were it, or of myself had Power or did or knew anything, or as if anything were mine or of me, or belonged to me, or were due to me or the like, I take unto myself somewhat of honour and glory, and do two evil things: First, I fall and go astray as aforesaid; Secondly, I touch God in His honour and take unto myself what belongeth to God only. For all that must be called good belongeth to none but to the true eternal Goodness which is God only, and whoso taketh it unto himself committeth unrighteousness and is against God.*

The subtlety of Satan as an angel of light comes just here, and we hear the saints, unwittingly and without any intention of doing it, taking the glory to themselves. To say a thing is the sure way to thinking it. That is why it is so necessary to testify to what Jesus Christ has done for us. A testimony gets hold of the mind as it has hold of the heart; but the same thing is true of the opposite, if we say a wrong thing often enough we begin to think it. The only way to be kept from taking glory to ourselves is to keep steadfastly faced by our Saviour and not by the needs of the people. Did you ever notice how God lets you go down when you trust good people? The best of men and women are but the best of men and women, the only good is God, and Jesus Christ always brings the soul face to face with God, and that is the one great thought we have to be soaked with. The spirit of covetousness is a flood, and when the Apostle Paul talked about the Spirit, his idea is of a flood, "Be [being] filled with the Spirit," invaded by the personal passionate Lover of God until we realise there is only one Good, and we have no time or inclination for any other kind of goodness. "In all the world there is none but Thee, my God, there is none but Thee." Are we there?

We will deal treacherously with the Bible records if we are not soaked in the revelation that God only is good. We will put the saints on the throne, not God. There is only one unshakeable goodness, and that is God. It takes time to get there because we will cling to things and to people. Those of us who ought to be princes and princesses with God cling to the shows of God's goodness instead of God Himself. The only influence that is to tell in a servant of God is God. Let people think what they like about you, but be careful that the last thought they get is God. When we have gone from them, there must be no beauty or fascination in us that makes them long for us, the only remembrance left must be, "That woman was true to God"; "That man was true to God."

*The quotations are from the book entitled Theologia Germanica.*

# III. The Philosophy of the Fall—II

By the Fall man not only died from God, but he fell into disunion with himself; that means it became possible for him to live in one of the three parts of his nature. We want to live a spiritual life, but we forget that that life has to work out in rational expression in our souls; or we want to live a clear life in the soul and forget altogether that we have a body and spirit; or else we want to live the life of a splendid animal and forget altogether the life of the soul and spirit. When a man is born again of the Spirit of God he is introduced to life with God and union with himself. The one thing essential to the new life is obedience to the Spirit of God Who has energised our spirits; that obedience must be complete in spirit, soul and body. We must not nourish one part of our being apart from the other parts.

## Margins of the Spirit (Galatians 5:19-24)

The margins of our spirit retain the damage done by the Fall, even after sanctification, and unless we are energised by the Spirit of God and continually draw our life from God, Satan will come in as an angel of light and deceive us, and the first way he does it is by habits of ecstasy.

### (a) Habits of Ecstasy

Habits of ecstasy, that is, the tendency to live a spiritual life before God apart from the rational life of our soul and the physical life of our body. In many a life the idea that creeps in slowly is that we must develop a spiritual life altogether apart from the rational and the physical life. God is never in that type of teaching. There are people we call naturally spiritual people who devote all their time to developing the spirit, forgetting altogether the rational life and the physical life. When we look at them or read about them they seem all right, spiritual and fine, but they lack the one marvellous stamp of the religion of Jesus Christ which keeps spirit, soul and body going on together. God never develops one part of our being at the expense of the other; spirit, soul and body are kept in harmony. Remember, our spirit does not go further than we bring our body. The Spirit of God always drives us out of the visionary, out of the excitable, out of the ecstasy stages, if we are inclined that way. This blind life of the spirit, a life that delights to live in the dim regions of the spirit, refusing to bring the leadings of the Holy Spirit into the rational life, gives occasion to supernatural forces that are not of God. It is impossible to guard our spirit, the only One Who can guard all its entrances is God. Never give way to spiritual ecstasy unless there is a chance of working it out rationally, check it every time. Nights and days of prayer and waiting on God may be a curse to our souls and an occasion for Satan. So always remember that the times we have in communion with God must be worked out in the soul and in the body.

### (b) Habits of Election of Days (Galatians 4:8-11)

The habits Paul refers to here are superstitious habits in which the mind fixes on "days, and months, and seasons, and years" (RV)—on certain days God will bless us, on other days He won't; if I am careful about this and that, it will bring me into the presence of God. The days, and months, and seasons, and years are appointed by God, but the Galatians were fixing on them altogether apart from God, and Paul says, "I am afraid of you, lest by any means I have bestowed labour upon you in vain" (RV). Nowadays superstition is growing again, and people are held in bondage to it. Are we in danger of fixing on means other than God for maintaining our spiritual life? Do we put the means of grace in the place of grace itself? If we make devotional habits the source from which we draw our life, God will put us through the discipline of upsetting those times. You say, "God does not upset them in other lives, why should He in mine?" Because you are putting them in the place of God. When you put God first you will easily get your times of communion, because God can entrust them to the soul who does not use them in an irrational way and give occasion to the enemy to enter in. When our spirit is awakened by God we must bring ourselves into subordination to the Spirit of God and not fly off at a tangent, fixing on days and seasons and ritual, thus giving a chance to the mysterious background of our life that we know nothing about but which the Bible reveals, and which Satan is on the watch for all the time.

The only soul Satan cannot touch is the soul whose spiritual life and rational life and physical life is hid with Christ in God; that soul is absolutely secure.

### (c) Habits of Enervation by Dreaming (Jude 8)

Ecstasy of spirit leads to external ritual in the rational life, and makes the bodily life spend its time in dreaming. The lassitude that creeps over an unhealthy soul produces the physical madness of hysteria. All animal magnetism, all the power of one person over another, and all the hysterics of self-pity that makes some people absolutely useless unless they are in the presence of certain other people, all spring from this source. It begins in a wrong relationship to God first; a real life with God was started, but instead of drawing the whole life from God and working it out through the body, the bodily life is spent in dreams, in fastings, in prayings, and slowly there develops a madness of the nerves, which is what hysteria really is. Hysteria is a physical morbid craving for sympathy from other people, which can go to such an extent that people cannot live apart from certain other people. There is no power of God in such lives. Hysteria is the actual nervous manifestation of fundamental self-pity, consequently it has been regarded for long by the medical world as a psycho-physical disease; it is more a disposition than a disease. In this domain we get the sympathy cures of Christian Science, i.e. a stronger personality coming in contact with a soul that has got out of touch with God through disobedience can soothe the hysteria of the nerves and inject a cure by its sympathy which has nothing to do with God or with the devil, but entirely to do with the influence of a strong personality over a weak one. Animal magnetism does not come from the devil, but remember that animal magnetism always gives occasion to the devil. In reading the records of French physicians, who used hypnotism in operating in the past more than they do now, case after case is recorded where a good-living physician used hypnotism but always stated his dread and dislike of it, simply because he found that he could never be sure what would happen to the person after the cure had been effected. And to-day we find over and over again that cures are genuine, the disease disappears, but there is a derangement in the life towards God and towards men. In every case of healing by God it comes through a child-like trust in Jesus Christ.

Any man or woman who is inclined to spend their time dreaming when they should be working out actually through the finger-tips what the Spirit of God is working in, is in danger of degenerating into those who "in their dreamings defile the flesh." God never allows a Christian to carry on his life in sections—so much time for study and meditation and so much for actual work; the whole life, spirit, soul and body must progress together.

Are you forming habits of ecstasy? Beware. Are you forming habits of ritual? habits of physical dreaming, wanting to get away from the active rush of things? Beware. When we get into the healthy life of God all the margins of spirit and soul and body are merged in a complete oneness with God. ". . . that ye may be filled unto all the fulness of God" (Ephesians 3:19 RV).

### (d) Habits of Envy (Proverbs 27:4)

Spiritual envy starts from having got something from God in the way of quickening and then trying to use it in our way, not God's. Spiritual envy is a terrible evil of the soul, and will always follow the tendency to develop a spiritual life apart from the rational life and the bodily life. All kinds of sour distempers will be ours spiritually, we shall be envious of people who are growing in their life with God in ways we are not, and we will have almost diabolical suggestions about them, suggestions we would never have got through our own unaided spirit. Spiritual envy is an awful possibility to any soul who does not obey the Spirit of God (cf. 1 Corinthians 13:4).

### (e) Habits of Emotions of Dread (Colossians 2:18)

If we separate the life of the spirit from the rational life, we experience emotions of dread, forebodings and spiritual nightmares in the soul, which are not imaginary but real. The cause is not always to be found in the physical condition, but in the margins of our spirit life. Remember that through the Fall man fell into dis-union, spirit, soul and body were separated from one another, that means we are liable to influences from God or from the devil. It is only when we get full of dread about life apart from God that we leave ourselves in His hands. Immediately we try to live a spiritual life with God and forget our soul and body, the devil pays attention to our body, and when we pay attention to our body he begins to get at our spirit, until we learn there is only one way to keep right— to live the life hid with Christ in God, then the very life and power of God garrisons all three domains, spirit, soul and body, but it depends on us whether we allow God to do it. God cannot garrison us if we try to live a spiritual life on a life of our own, or if we go off on emotions in our rational life. God never garrisons us in bits. Whenever marrings come to our lives it is because we have got twisted off somewhere, we are not living in simple, full, child-like union with God, handing the keeping of our lives over to Him and being carefully careless about everything saving our relationship to Him; keep that right, and He will guard every avenue. "Kept by the power of God."

### (f) Habits of Exceptional "Drugging" (Jude 12-13)

There are hidden perils in our life with God whenever we disobey Him. If we are not obeying God physically we experience a craving for drugs, not only physical drugs out of a bottle, but drugs in certain types of meetings and certain types of company— anything that keeps away the realisation that the habits of the bodily life are not in accordance with what is God's will. If in the providence of God, obedience to God takes me into contact with people and surroundings that are wrong and bad, I may be perfectly certain that God will guard me; but if I go there out of curiosity, God does not guard me, and the tendency is to "drug" it over—"I went with a good idea to try and find out about these things." Well, you plainly had no business to go, and you know you had no business to go because the Spirit of God is absolutely honest. The whole thing starts from disobedience on a little point. We wanted to utilise God's grace for our own purposes, to use God's gifts for our own reasoning out of things in a particular way.

### (g) Habits of Enmity (Romans 8:7)

The carnal mind is a dangerous power alongside the Spirit of God in our personality before identification with Jesus Christ in His death and resurrection is reached. When a man has received the Holy Spirit, the watching of Satan is keen, his whole desire is to split up the personality. "For the flesh lusteth against the Spirit, and the Spirit against the flesh; for these are contrary the one to the other" (Galatians 5:17 RV). The carnal mind is enmity against God, and it is the carnal mind which connects us with the body of sin of which Satan is the head, and of which there is ultimately to be a new manifestation (see 2 Thessalonians 2:3). Every soul who enters into the experience of entire sanctification limits the body of sin, consequently the great yearning eagerness of the preaching of the Gospel is to get God's children to the place of sanctification where spirit, soul and body are one, one personality absolutely ruled by God, where the life of the spirit is instantly manifested in the life of the soul and body (see 1 Thessalonians 5:23). If this place of entire sanctification is not reached, there is always that in us which has a strong affinity with the devil, and this is the remarkable thing, we never knew it before we were introduced into the kingdom of God by the initial experience of regeneration; but we find after a while the strong lustful hate of something in us against what the Spirit God has put in, and the lust is for one thing—I want to dominate this personality.

### (h) Habits of Earnest Devotions (Colossians 2:20-23)

Have we any helps to keep us living a godly life? That is the risk. Slowly and surely God will purify our lives from props that separate us from Him. Immediately the means of grace are taken to be grace itself, they become a direct hindrance to our life with God. The means are simply scaffolding for the time being, and as long as they are in their right place they are an assistance, immediately we put them as the source, we give occasion to the enemy. Have we helped ourselves in work for God from any other source than God? "Ye are complete in Him" (Colossians 2:10).

### (i) Habits of Extraordinary Defying (2 Thessalonians 2:9-12)

A spiritual man or woman going astray can use the extraordinary powers awakened by the Spirit of God against God. The only safeguard, and it is an absolute safeguard, is to live the life hid with Christ in God. The life that steadily refuses to think from its right to itself, that steadily refuses to trust its own insight, is the only life that Satan cannot touch. Watch every time you get to a tight feeling spiritually, to a dry feeling rationally, to a hindered feeling physically, it is the Spirit of God's quiet warning that you should repair to the heavenly places in Christ Jesus. There is never any fear for the life that is hid with Christ in God, but there is not only fear, but terrible danger, for the life unguarded by God. "He that dwelleth in the secret place of the Most High"—once there, and although God's providence should take you into hell itself, you are as safe and secure as Almighty God can keep you.

# IV. THE PHILOSOPHY OF DISCERNMENT

A philosopher is a lover of wisdom, and spiritual philosophy means the love of wisdom not only in our heart life, but in our heads—the last place a Christian gets to. Usually we leave our heads barren, we simply use our brains to explain our heart's experience. That is necessary, but we have to let our brains be guided by the Holy Spirit into thinking a great many things we have not experienced. That is, we are committed to Jesus Christ's view of everything, and if we only allow our brains to dwell on what we have experienced, we shut ourselves off from a great deal we ought to be exercised in. Our heart experience always outstrips our head statement, and when the experience begins to be stated explicitly, our heart witnesses to it—"Why I know that, but I never realised before how it worked." Discernment is the power to interpret what we see and hear.

## The Path of Discernment

> *For without Me ye can do nothing. (John 15:5)*
>
> *. . . man's knowledge should be so clear and perfect that he should acknowledge of a truth (that in himself he neither hath nor can do any good thing, and that none of his knowledge, wisdom and art, his will, love and good works do come from himself, nor are of man, nor of any creature, but) that all these are of the eternal God from whom they all proceed.*

Have I learned to think what the testimony of my heart makes me state? We all say this kind of thing—"I know that in me . . . dwelleth no good thing," but do we *think* it? Do we really think what Jesus has taught us to know in our hearts, that apart from Him we can do nothing? We all believe it, but do we think it? Over and over again God has to take us into desert places spiritually where there is no conscious experience at all. We have probably all had this in our experience—we have had a grand time of living communion with God, we know we are sanctified, the witness of the Spirit has proved it over and over again, then all of a sudden there falls a dearth, no life, no quickness; there is no degeneration, no backsliding, but an absolute dearth. This may be the reason—

the Lord is wanting to take us to a desert place apart that we may get to this path of discernment. All the noisy things that fret our lives when we are spiritual come because we have not discerned what we know in our hearts.

### (a) The Discipline of Negatives (1 Corinthians 4:7)

Paul is talking about natural gifts as well as spiritual. "What hast thou that thou didst not receive? but if thou didst receive it, why dost thou glory, as if thou hadst not received it?" (RV). Have we learned to think when we see someone endowed with natural gifts, such as a fine voice, or a good brain, or any of the gifts of genius, that every one of those gifts has been received, therefore they cannot be consecrated? You cannot consecrate what is not yours. In thinking we do not really go along the scriptural lines our hearts go on. Watch your heart in relationship to God, you recognise that you cannot consecrate yourself to God: you *give* yourself to God, and yet in thinking we go along the line of consecrating our gifts to God. We have to get rid altogether of the idea that our gifts are ours, they are not, gifts are gifts, and we have to be so given over to God that we never think of our gifts, then God can let His own life flow through us. The discipline of negatives is the hardest discipline in the spiritual life, and if you are going through it you ought to shout "Hallelujah," for it is a sign that God is getting your mind and heart where the mind and heart of Jesus Christ was.

Spiritual gifts must be dealt with in the same way as natural gifts. Spiritual gifts are not glorified gifts, they are the gift of the Spirit. "Now there are diversities of gifts, but the same Spirit." None of the gifts Paul mentions in 1 Corinthians 12:8-11 are natural gifts. The danger is to say, "How highly favoured I must be if God gives me this great gift"; "what a wonderful person I must be." We never talk like that, but the slightest thought that looks upon the gifts of the Spirit as a favour to us is the first thing that will take us out of the central point of Jesus Christ's teaching. Never look at the work of God in and through you; never look at the way God uses you in His service; immediately you do, you put your mind away from where Jesus Christ wants to get it. Gifts are *gifts,* not graces.

### (b) The Development of Nobility (2 Corinthians 3:5-6)

Paul is calling his own mind to a halt in order to explain to the Corinthian Church why what he says and does comes with authority. "Our sufficiency is from God; Who also made us sufficient as ministers of a new covenant" (RV). If you are right with God, you will be amazed at what other people get in the way of real spiritual help out of what you say; but never think about it. The temptation comes all along to say, "It is because I brooded that God gave me that thought." The right attitude is to keep the mind absolutely concentrated on God and never get off on the line of how you are being used by Him. Even in the choicest of saints there is the danger. Whenever you feel inclined to say, "Well, of course that was not me, that was God," beware! you ought never to be in the place where you can think it. The teaching of Jesus is, "Be absorbed with Me, and out of you will flow rivers of living water" If we are paying attention to the Source, rivers of living water will pour out of us, but immediately we stop paying attention to the Source, the outflow begins to dry up. We have nothing to do with our "usability," but only with our relationship to Jesus Christ, nothing must be allowed to come in between.

Have we allowed this path of discernment to be trodden by our feet? Are we beginning to see where we are being led, viz. to the place where we are rooted and grounded in God? The one essential thing is to live the life hid with Christ in God.

## The Pain of Deliverance

> And Jesus called a little child unto Him . . . and said, . . . Except ye . . . become as little children . . . (Matthew 18:2-3)

> For when the vain imagination and ignorance are turned into an understanding and knowledge of the truth, the claiming of anything for our own will cease of itself.

A healthy man does not know what health is: a sick man knows what health is, because he has lost it; and a saint rightly related to God does not know what the will of God is because he *is* the will of God. A disobedient soul knows what the will of God is because he has disobeyed. The illustration Jesus gives to His disciples of a saintly life is a little child. Jesus did not put up a child as an ideal, but to show them that ambition has no place whatever in the disposition of a Christian. The life of a child is unconscious in its fullness of life, and the source of its life is implicit love. To be made children over again causes pain because we have to reconstruct our mental ways of looking at things after God has dealt with our heart experience. Some of us retain our old ways of looking at things, and the deliverance is painful. Paul urges that we allow the pain—"Let this mind be in you, which was also in Christ Jesus"; "bringing into captivity every thought to the obedience of Christ." It is hard to do it. In the beginning we are so anxious—"Lord, give me a message for this meeting," until we learn that if we live in the centre of God's will, He will give us messages when He likes and withhold them when He likes. We try to help God help Himself to us; we have to get out of the way and God will help Himself to our lives in every detail. Have we learned to form the mind of Christ by the pain of deliverance till we know we are drawing on Him for everything? Are we sacrificing our holy selves to the will of Jesus as He did to the will of His Father? Are we beginning to speak what God wants us to speak because we are submitting our intelligence to Him? "The Son can do nothing of Himself." Our Lord never allowed such a thought as, "I have done that," in His mind. Have we spiritual discernment like that? If not, remember what the Apostle James says, "If any of you lack wisdom, let him ask of God, that giveth to all men liberally and upbraideth not; and it shall be given him."

### (a) The Plunge into God (1 Corinthians 13:8-10)

> Now when a man duly perceiveth these things in himself he and the creature fall behind, and he doth not call anything his own, and the less he taketh this knowledge unto himself the more perfect doth it become. So also is it with the will and

*love, and desire, and the like. For the less we call these things our own, the more perfect and noble and Godlike do they become, and the more we think them our own, the baser and less pure and perfect do they become.*

The only way to learn to swim is to take the plunge, sink or swim; that is exactly the idea here. Will I cut loose from all moorings and plunge straight into God? It is what the New Testament is continually urging—"Let go." Life goes on in a series of coveting the best gifts, but, Paul says, "a still more excellent way shew I unto you" (RV)—take an absolute plunge into the love of God, and when you are there you will be amazed at your foolishness for not getting there before. It is not the question of the surrender of a soul for sanctification, but the unreserved surrender of a sanctified soul to God. We are so reserved where we ought to be unreserved, and so unreserved where we ought to be reserved. We ought never to be reserved towards God but utterly open, perfectly one with Him all through. After the experience of sanctification we have to present our sanctified self to God, and one of the greatest difficulties in doing this is considering the conditions other people say we have to observe. "They themselves, . . . comparing themselves with themselves, are without understanding" (RV). Watch how tied up we are with other people's notions of what we should be. The only way to get rid of it all is to take this plunge into the love of God. We have to form the mind of Christ until we are absorbed in Him and take no account of the evil done to us. No love on earth can do this but the love of God.

### (b) The Participation in Godliness (Philippians 3:7-8)

*We must cast all things from us, and strip ourselves of them; we must refrain from claiming anything for our own.*

". . . for Whom I suffered the loss of all things" (RV). To experience the loss of all things for anyone but Jesus Christ is mental suicide. Read what Our Lord said to the rich young ruler—""Sell whatsoever thou hast, . . . and come, follow Me—"Reduce yourself until you are a mere conscious man, and then give that manhood to Me"; and we read that "his countenance fell at the saying, and he went away sorrowful: for he was one that had great possessions" (RV). Do you possess a reputation as a Christian worker? That will be in the way when the Lord speaks to you. Are you rich in the consciousness that you are somebody spiritually? That will be in the way. You must first estimate and then experience the loss of all things and cast yourself on Jesus, then participation in godliness will be yours as it never has been.

> *When we do this, we shall have the best, fullest, clearest and noblest knowledge that a man can have, and also the noblest and purest love, will and desire; for then these will be all of God alone. It is much better that they should be God's than the creature's.*

The oneness Jesus Christ prayed for in John 17 is the oneness of identity, not of union. "I and My Father are one," and by the Atonement our Lord brings us into identity with Himself—"that they may be one, even as We are one."

## The Plane of Delight (2 Corinthians 4:16-18)

> *While we look . . . at the things which are not seen.*
> *(2 Corinthians 4:18)*

> *But if our inward man were to make a leap and spring into the Perfect, we should find and taste how that the Perfect is without measure, number or end, better and nobler than all which is imperfect and in part, and the Eternal above the temporal or perishable, and the foundation and source above all that floweth or can ever flow from it.*

When we think of being delivered from sin, of being filled with the Spirit, we say, "Oh, I shall never get there, it is only for exceptional people like the Apostle Paul"; but when by God's grace we get there we find it is the easiest place to live; it is not a mountain-peak, but a flat tableland of delight with plenty of room for everyone. "And I pray God your whole spirit and soul and body be preserved blameless"—that is not the life we are to live hereafter, but the life God would have us live now; most of us are far too diffident about getting there.

### (a) The Altitude of Love

> . . . the greatest of these is love. (1 Corinthians 13:13 RV)

> A Master called Bætius said, "It is of sin that we do not love that which is Best." He hath spoken the truth. That which is best should be the dearest of all things to us.

Is it? Sometimes we crave for something less than the best, beware! We ought to love the most what is best. The spirit of God in us can teach us how to love the best, through faith, through knowledge, through everything till we are altogether in love with God, in absolute harmony with Him, absorbed in the one great purpose of God.

> And in our love of it, neither helpfulness nor unhelpfulness, advantage nor injury, gain nor loss, honour nor dishonour, praise nor blame, nor anything of the kind should be regarded.

1 Corinthians 13 is not an ideal, it is an identification which makes the ideal possible. Never put the ideal where the Spirit of God does not put it. The ideal comes after the identification.

### (b) The Atmosphere of Life

> But the fruit of the Spirit is love. . . (Galatians 5:22)

> Now that creature in which the Eternal Good, most manifesteth itself shineth forth, worketh, is most known and loved, is the best, and that wherein the Eternal Good is least manifested is the least good of all creatures.

In days gone by we all used to love the creatures that exhibit reflections of the Eternal Good—honour and courage and strength, but when we are made one with Jesus Christ we find we love the creatures that exhibit the fruit of the Spirit. A great alteration has come over our outlook; God is altering the thing that matters.

*Therefore when we have to do with the creatures and hold converse with them, and take note of their diverse qualities, the best creatures must always be the dearest to us, and we must cleave to them, and unite ourselves to them.*

"What communion hath light with darkness?" The education God puts His children through in life is, "first that which is natural; then that which is spiritual," until we are rooted and grounded in Him, then there is no danger evermore to that life. It is always better further on—through the natural to the spiritual. No wonder the counsel of the Spirit through the writer to the Hebrews is "Ye have need of patience."

*The quotations are from the book entitled Theologia Germanica.*

# V. The Philosophy of Following Our Lord

*First, man must consider the teaching and the life of Jesus Christ, for He hath taught poverty and lived it. And a man should follow the teaching and the life, if he wisheth to be perfect, for He saith, "Whoso loveth Me keepeth My commandments and My counsels, and heareth My word."*

In every profession under heaven the great ambition of the natural heart is to be perfect. When Jesus Christ was faced with a splendid specimen of a young man, He said, "If you would be perfect, I will tell you what to do."

"If a man love Me, he will keep My words: and My Father will love him, and We will come unto him, and make our abode with him." The whole outcome of following Jesus is expressed for us in these words, viz. that the Trinity, Father, Son, and Holy Ghost, will come and make Their abode with the man who loves Jesus and keeps His word. As long as the devil can keep us terrified of thinking, he will always limit the work of God in our souls.

## The Way of the Follower Negative

*If any man will come after Me, let him deny himself, and take up his cross daily, and follow Me. (Luke 9:23)*

The word "deny" embraces what the Apostle Paul meant when he said "mortify therefore," or, make dead, "your members which are upon the earth" (Colossians 3:5).

### (a) Infirmity-Sins

*For if ye live after the flesh, ye shall die: but if ye through the Spirit do mortify the deeds of the body, ye shall live. (Romans 8:13)*

*It might now be said, What is man in his selfhood, that he must deny, if he wisheth to follow after Christ? Man's selfhood consisteth in four things. First, his frailty, and that he falleth into sins; and this he must needs set aside; he must die to his defects and sins, and mortify himself.*

The disposition in us is either implanted naturally through the first Adam, or implanted supernaturally through the last Adam by regeneration and sanctification. We breed our temperament out of the disposition that is in us. If we are going to follow Jesus, we must do to death infirmity-sins. God cannot do it, we have to do it ourselves. Satan takes occasion of the frailty of the bodily temple and says, "Now you know you cannot do that, you are so infirm, you cannot concentrate your mind," etc. Never allow bodily infirmities to hinder you obeying the commands of Jesus. Paul says, "But I keep under my body, and bring it into subjection." "I buffet [bruise, mg] my body, and bring it into bondage" (RV). Through the Atonement God deals with the wrong disposition in us, then He gives us the glorious privilege of making our bodies "instruments of righteousness unto God."

### (b) Inordinate Affection

> *Mortify therefore your members which are upon the earth; . . . inordinate affection. . . . (Colossians 3:5)*
>
> Secondly, he is inclined to creatures. For man is inclined by nature to his like, and he must kill nature, and must withdraw from creatures, for God and creatures are opposites. And therefore he who wisheth to have God must leave creatures. For the soul is so narrow that God and the creature cannot dwell together in her; and therefore if God is to dwell in thy soul, the creature must remain without.

In Colossians 3:5 Paul is describing an unsanctified man, but the same man sanctified is inclined to creatures rather than to the Creator. Watch the hard things Jesus says about father, mother, wife, children, our own life (see Luke 14:26); He says if we are going to follow Him, these must be on the outside of the central citadel. The central citadel must be God and God alone. When once we are willing to "do to death" our clinging to creatures, which in certain supreme calls comes between ourselves and God, Jesus says we will receive an hundredfold, because immediately we are rightly related to God He can trust us with creature relationships without fear of inordinateness. With the majority of us these relationships are cut off, not by our own doing, God has to do it for us; He has to come with strange providences and cut them off, because we have professed that we are going to follow Jesus. We forget that sanctification is only the beginning; the one purpose of sanctification is that Jesus might be "marvelled at in all them that believed."

### (c) Inveterate Luxury

> But I keep under my body, and bring it into subjection: lest that by any means, when I have preached to others, I myself should be a castaway. (1 Corinthians 9:27)

> The third point is, that man to part from selfhood should drop all sensual delight, for he must die to this and kill it in himself if he wisheth to have God's comfort. As St. Bernard saith, "The comfort of God is so noble that no one receiveth it who seeketh comfort elsewhere."

The natural life in a sanctified man or woman is neither moral nor immoral, it is the gift God has given the saint to sacrifice on the altar of love to God. Jesus Christ had a natural body, it was not a sin for Him to be hungry, but it would have been a sin for Him to satisfy that hunger when God had told Him not to, and Satan came to Him when He had fasted forty days and forty nights, and was an hungred, and said, "Satisfy that hunger now." The body we have is not sinful in itself; if it were, it would be untrue to say that Jesus Christ was sinless. Paul's words have reference to the fact that our body has been ruled by a sinful disposition, a disposition which simply means I am going to find my sustaining in creature comforts. After we are sanctified we have the same body, but it is ruled by a new disposition, and we have to sacrifice our natural life to God even as Jesus did, so that we make the natural life spiritual by a series of direct moral choices.

### (d) Intellectual Intemperance

*And lest I should be exalted above measure . . . through the abundance of the revelations . . . (2 Corinthians 12:7)*

*The fourth thing a man must let go if he wisheth to follow Christ, is spiritual natural comforts, which are generated in man, by detecting the distinction between spiritual and natural knowledge. . . . Whoever tarries by this natural rational delight, hinders himself from the supernatural delight which God in His grace imparteth to the soul.*

Intellectual intemperance is a great snare to a saint. Bodily fasting is child's play compared to the determined fasting from the intellectual apprehension of the teachings of Jesus that goes beyond what we are living out. The characteristic of many spiritual people to-day is intellectual intemperance, fanatical intoxication with the things of God, wild exuberance, an unlikeness to the sanity of Jesus in the very ways of God. There is a danger in the enjoyment of the delights and the power that come to us through Jesus Christ's salvation without lifting the life into keeping with His teaching, especially in spiritual people whose minds have never been disciplined and they wander off into all kinds of vagaries. That accounts for the distinction we find between spiritual sincerity and spiritual reality.

All this is the negative side of following our Lord. Have we told Jesus we will follow Him? Are we prepared to do our part in keeping under the body for one purpose only, that we may learn the fellowship of following? Are we beginning to realise that until we are born again the teachings of Jesus are simple; after we are born again they become growingly difficult, and we find clouds and darkness are round about the things we thought we knew perfectly well once, and following our Lord is one of these things?

## The Way of the Fellowship Positive

*And he that taketh not his cross, and followeth after Me, is not worthy of Me. He that findeth his*

*life shall lose it: and he that loseth his life for My sake*
*shall find it. (Matthew 10:38-39)*


It is possible to be grossly selfish in absorbing the salvation of Jesus, to enjoy all its benedictions, and never follow Him one step. So Jesus says, "If any man would follow Me, this is the way"— "let him deny himself, and take up his cross daily, and follow Me."

### (a) Working Virtue from God

> *. . . for as ye have yielded your members servants to*
> *uncleanness and to iniquity unto iniquity; even so*
> *now yield your members servants to righteousness*
> *unto holiness. (Romans 6:19)*

> *First, man should kill sin in himself through virtue; for just*
> *as man is removed from God by sin must he be brought nigh*
> *again unto God by virtue . . . but let no one believe that he is*
> *free from sins, unless he hath taken unto himself all the virtues.*

The positive side is this—that we work all the virtues of Jesus in and through our members, but this can only be done when all self-reliance has come to an end (cf. 2 Corinthians 1:9). Our natural virtues are remnants of what God created man to be, not promises of what he is going to be. The natural virtues cannot be patched up to come anywhere near God's demands, and the sign that God is at work in us is that He corrupts our confidence in the natural virtues. It is simply an amplification of the old Gospel hymn—

> *Nothing in my hand I bring,*
> *Simply to Thy Cross I cling!*


### (b) Willing Poverty for God

> *For ye know the grace of our Lord Jesus Christ,*
> *that, though He was rich, yet for your sakes He*
> *became poor, that ye through His poverty might be*
> *rich. (2 Corinthians 8:9)*

> *The second thing that man must shun is the love for creatures. Poverty of spirit is a going out of yourself and out of everything earthly. Thereby he despiseth creatures, is despised by them, and is thus set free. A truly poor man taketh nothing from creatures, but all from God, be it bodily or spiritual. God alone will be the Giver.*

To be willingly poor for God is to strip myself of all things for the sake of Jesus Christ. One of the greatest snares is built on what is really a great truth, viz. that every man has Christ in himself. The pernicious use that is made of that statement is that therefore man draws power from himself. Never! Jesus Christ never drew power from Himself: He drew it always from without Himself, viz. from His Father. "The Son can do nothing of Himself" (John 5:19, see John 5:30). Beware of being rich spiritually on earth, only be rich spiritually in heaven. Jesus said to the rich young ruler, "If you will strip yourself and have no riches here, you will lay up for yourself treasure in heaven Treasure in heaven." is faith that has been tried (cf. Revelation 3:18). Immediately we begin to have fellowship with Jesus we have to live the life of faith at all costs; it may be bitter to begin with, but afterwards it is ineffably and indescribably sweet—willing poverty for God, a determined going outside myself and every earthly thing.

### (c) Watchful Purity for God

> *Whosoever is born of God doth not commit sin; for His seed remaineth in him: and he cannot sin, because he is born of God. (1 John 3:9)*

> *But who knoweth, wilt thou ask, if he have all virtues? I answer to this like John, who saith, "Whosoever is born of God cannot sin." For in the same moment in which God the Father begetteth His Son in the soul, sins and all unlikeness disappear, and all virtues are born in her in a likeness to God.*

According to that statement of the Apostle John no one is free from sin unless he is possessed of all the virtues. The Apostle is not teaching sinless perfection; he is teaching perfect sinlessness, which is a different matter. If as sanctified souls we walk in the light, as

God is in the light, the revelation is that through the Atonement "the blood of Jesus Christ His Son cleanseth us from all sin." That does not mean cleansing from all sin in our consciousness; if it did, it would produce hypocrisy. Any number of people are not conscious of sin, but it does not follow that they are cleansed from all sin. It is not our consciousness that is referred to, but the consciousness God has of us; what we are conscious of is walking in the light with nothing to hide. The outcome of following our Lord is a holiness of character so that God sees nothing to censure because the life of His Son is working out in every particular. Our main idea is to keep steadfastly in the blazing light of God so that He can exhibit the virtues of Jesus through us unhindered. "If ye love Me, ye will keep My commandments" (RV). How many of them? All of them. Then, says Jesus, "We will come unto him, and make Our abode with him"—in heaven? No, here.

### (d) Wonderful Passion for God

> Forasmuch then as Christ hath suffered for us in the flesh, arm yourselves likewise with the same mind: for he that hath suffered in the flesh hath ceased from sin; that he no longer should live the rest of his time in the flesh to the lusts of men, but to the will of God. (1 Peter 4:1-2)

> . . . and whoso would eat its fruit (the fruit of the holy cross) with profit must break it off from the cross by steadfast internal contemplation of the Passion of Our Lord.

> All on the cross is full of fruit, and more than all tongues could in truth proclaim. Nay, angels' tongues could not describe the overflowing grace that is there hidden in the Passion of our Lord. Blessed are those who have found this treasure.

Steady contemplation of the Passion of our Lord will "do to death" everything that is not of God. It is only after a long while of going on with God and steady contemplation of the Cross that we begin to understand its meaning. "To day shalt thou be with Me in paradise" is said at only one place, viz. at the Cross.

This is not a message about our salvation and sanctification, but about the outcome of salvation and sanctification in our implicit life, i.e. where we live it and cannot speak it. Jesus said, "If any man would be My disciple . . ." not, "If any man would be saved and sanctified." "If any man will be My disciple—those are the conditions." Jesus Christ always talked about discipleship with an "If." We are at perfect liberty to toss our spiritual head and say, "No, thank you, that is a bit too stern for me," and the Lord will never say a word, we can do exactly what we like. He will never plead, but the opportunity is there, "If . . ."

After all, it is the great stern call of Jesus that fascinates men and women quicker than anything. It is not the gospel of being saved from hell and enjoying heaven that attracts men, saving in a very shallow mood; it is Christ crucified that attracts men; Jesus said so—"I, if I be lifted up from the earth, will draw all men unto Me." Jesus Christ never attracts us by the unspeakable bliss of Paradise; He attracts us by an ugly beam. We talk about getting down to the depths of a man's soul: Jesus Christ is the only One Who ever did. If once a man has heard the appeal of Jesus from the Cross, he begins to find there is something there that answers the cry of the human heart and the problem of the whole world. What we have to do as God's servants is to lift up Christ crucified. We can either do it as gramophones, or as those who are in fellowship with Him.

Many of us have heard Jesus Christ's first "Follow Me"—to a life of liberty and joy and gladness; how many of us have heard the second "Follow Me"—"deny your right to yourself and 'do to death' in yourself everything that never was in Me"?

*The quotations are from the book entitled The Following of Christ, by John Tauler.*

# VI. THE PHILOSOPHY OF GODLINESS

*Verily, verily, I say unto you, He that believeth on Me, the works that I do shall he do also; and greater works than these shall he do; because I go unto My Father. John 14:12*

## The Way of the Working of God

> *Then said they unto Him, What shall we do that we might work the works of God? Jesus answered and said unto them, This is the work of God, that ye believe on Him Whom He hath sent. (John 6:28-29)*

> *There are two kinds of work in God—a working within and a working outwardly. The working inward is God's being and nature, the outward working is the creature. . . . God worketh in souls that He may bring them to the first origin from which they have flowed, for by their works they cannot go in again.*

These words of Jesus sum up the whole mystery of the work of grace, viz. that to "work the works of God" we must stop working and let God work. "This is the work of God, that ye believe. . . ."Un-belief is the most active thing on earth; it is negative on God's side, not on ours. Un-belief is a fretful, worrying, questioning, annoying, self-centred spirit. To believe is to stop all this and let God work.

### (a) The Working Master

> *. . . work out your own salvation with fear and trembling, for it is God which worketh in you both to will and to do of His good pleasure. (Philippians 2:12-13)*

> *If man is to come to God, he must be empty of all work and let God work alone. . . . Now, all that God willeth to have from us is that we be inactive, and let Him be the working Master.*

Paul does not say, Work out something that will tell for your salvation; he says, Work out in the expression of your life the salvation God has worked in. If we think for a moment we shall soon know how much we are saved—What does our tongue say? what kind of things do our ears like to listen to? what kind of bodily associates do we like to be with? These things will always tell not only other people but ourselves what kind of salvation God has worked in. In regeneration God works us into relation with Himself that by our bodily expression we may prove Whose we are. If you are trying to be a Christian it is a sure sign you are not one. Fancy trying to be the daughter of your mother! you cannot help being her daughter. But try and be the daughter of someone else's mother! Unless God has worked in us we shall hinder Him all the time by trying to be His children; we cannot, we have to be born from above (rv mg) by the will of God first, be regenerated; then our working is not working to help God, it is working to let God express through us what He has done in us so that we may prove we are the children of our Father in heaven (see Matthew 5:43-48).

So many of us put prayer and work and consecration in place of the working of God; we make ourselves the workers. God is the Worker, we work out what He works in. Spirituality is what God is after, not religiosity. The great snare in religion without genuine spirituality is that people ape being good when they are absolutely mean. There is no value whatever in religious externals, the only thing that is of value is spiritual reality, and this is spiritual reality—that I allow God to work in me to will and to do of His good pleasure, and then work out what He has worked in, being carefully careless about everything saving my relationship to God.

## (b) The Workable Medium

> If a man abide not in Me, he is cast forth as a branch, and is withered. (John 15:6)

> If we were altogether inactive we should be perfect men. For all that is good is the work of God, and if God does not work it, it is not good.

I wonder how many of us are living on the virtues of our grandparents! The natural virtues are remnants of what the original creation of man once was, they are not promises of what man is going to be; what man is going to be is seen in the life of Jesus Christ. The workable medium is man. God takes as the medium of working the stuff we are made of, and all He requires is for us to be inactive and let Him work. When once we are rightly related to God through the Atonement we will be inactive and not in the way of His working in us as He worked in Jesus; consequently we shall be able to work out in our natural life all that God wills. It is the old twist, we will try to do what God alone can do, and then we mourn before God because He won't do what we alone can do. We put up sighing petitions—"I have tried to be good"; "I have tried to sanctify myself." All that is the work of God, and the best thing to do is to stop trying and let God do it. What we have to do, and what God cannot do, is to work out what He has worked in. We try to do God's work for Him, and God has to wait until we are passive enough to let Him work in us. To believe in Jesus means retiring and letting God take the mastership inside. That is all God asks of us. Have we ever got into the way of letting God work, or are we so amazingly important that we really wonder in our nerves and ways what the Almighty does before we are up in the morning! We are so certain we know what is right, and if we don't always keep at it God cannot get on. Compare that view with the grand, marvellous working of God in the life of the Lord Jesus. Our Lord did not work for God; He said, "The Father that dwelleth in Me, He doeth the works." Have we any faith in God at all? Do we really expect God to work in us the good pleasure of His will, or do we expect He will only do it as we pray and plead and sacrifice? All these things shut the door to God working. What we have to ask away from, to knock at, to seek through, are these pressing strivings of our own—

*When we stay our feeble efforts,*
*And from struggling cease,*
*Unconditional surrender*
*Brings us God's own peace.*

—a doctrine easily travestied, but a doctrine God never safeguards. The whole basis of modern Christian work is the great impulsive desire to evade concentration on God. We will work for Him any day rather than let Him work in us. When a man or woman realises what God does work in them through Jesus Christ, they become almost lunatic with joy in the eyes of the world. It is this truth we are trying to state, viz. the realisation of the wonderful salvation of God.

## (c) The Worker's Manner

> *And now abideth faith, hope, charity, these three; but the greatest of these is charity. (1 Corinthians 13:13)*

> *How is a man to know if his work is of himself or from God? Shortly be it said; there are three supernatural divine virtues, Faith, Hope, and Love or Charity; whatever increaseth virtues is from God, but what diminisheth them is a sign that it is the work of man. . . . For what man worketh of himself, he applieth to himself and to time . . . but what God worketh, draweth a man away from himself to eternity, and this increaseth Faith, Hope, and Charity.*

How much of faith, hope, and love is worked in us when we try to convince somebody else? It is not our business to convince other people, that is the insistence of a merely intellectual, unspiritual life. The Spirit of God will do the convicting when we are in the relationship where we simply convey God's word. We exploit the word of God in order to fit it into some view of our own that we have generated; but when it comes to the great calm peace and rest of the Lord Jesus, we can easily test where we are. To "rest in the Lord" is the perfection of inward activity. In the ordinary reasoning of man it means sitting with folded arms and letting God do everything; in reality it is being so absolutely stayed on God that we are free to do the active work of men without fuss. The times God works most wonderfully are the times we never think about it. When we work of ourselves we always connect things with time.

"What is the good of faith, hope and love when I have to earn my living?" Compare that outlook with what Jesus says in the Sermon on the Mount—"Seek ye first the kingdom of God, and His righteousness; and all these things shall be added unto you." It means on our part a continual carelessness about everything but that one thing. The great curse of modern Christianity is that people will not be careless about things they have no right to be careful about, and they will not let God make them careful about their relationship to Him. Sum it up for yourself—what do you think about most, not on the surface, but in the deep centre of your centre? What is the real basal thought of your life—"what ye shall eat, or what ye shall drink; . . . what ye shall put on"? None of us are so stupid or lacking in cunning as to say we do think of these things: but if we think of what will happen to "all these things" if we put God first, we know where we are, God is not first. If He is first you know you can never think of anything He will forget.

## The Way of the Working of the Godly

> *Therefore if any man be in Christ, he is a new creature; . . . and all things are of God. (2 Corinthians 5:17-18)*

> *What is the divine work? It is twofold, what God worketh in the soul, one the work of grace, the other essential and divine. By the work of grace man is prepared for the essential . . . by grace God maketh man well-pleasing, it driveth him away from all defective things on to virtue, so that with it he obtaineth all virtues.*

The only sign that we are new creations (RV MG) in Christ Jesus is that we know all things are of God. When we are in difficult circumstances, when we are hard up, when friends slander us, to whom do we go? If we know that "all things are of God," then we certainly are new creations in Christ Jesus. The things that upset the external life reveal where we live. If we are in Christ the whole basis of our goings is God, not conceptions of God, not ideas of God, but God Himself. We do not need any more ideas about God, the world is full of ideas about God, they are all worthless, because the ideas of God in anyone's head are of no more use than our own ideas. What we need is a real God, not more ideas about Him. Immediately we get a real God we find that "old things are passed away; behold, all things are become new"; we are so absolutely one with God that we never think of saying we are, the whole life is hid with Christ in God.

## (a) The Experimental Virtue

> For by grace are ye saved through faith; and that not of yourselves: it is the gift of God. (Ephesians 2:8)

God worketh through His grace in man, when He draweth him away from sin and leadeth him on to virtue, if man leaveth sin and exerciseth virtue, this is a grace of God.

When we are first born again of the Spirit and become rightly related to God, the whole set of our life is along God's line, other people looking at us know how marvellously God has transformed us; we do things and wonder why we do them. That is experimental virtue, but it is accidental, that is, the expression in our life is that of spiritual innocence not of spiritual holiness yet; then slowly and surely the Holy Spirit leads on to the next thing—the essence of virtue.

## (b) The Essence of Virtue

> My little children, of whom I travail in birth again until Christ be formed in you. (Galatians 4:19)

The second work that God worketh in the soul is essential; when man cometh to this that he hath obtained all accidental virtue, and so now arriveth at the essence of virtue, then God worketh all virtue in him in an essential way, namely, the Heavenly Father begetteth His Son in the soul, and this birth raiseth the spirit above all created things into God.

"Until Christ"—not Jesus Christ, but Christ, the Son of God, Who was Incarnate once as a Man called Jesus Christ—"until Christ be formed in you." No wonder Paul talks about "the riches of the glory of this mystery; . . . which is Christ in you, the hope of glory." This is not an innocent state, it is a holy state, the very essence of the life is holy, and as we draw on His resurrection life, the life of Jesus is manifested in our mortal flesh.

### (c) The Essential Vision

> But God . . . hath raised us up together, and made us sit together in heavenly places in Christ Jesus. (Ephesians 2:4, 6)
>
> Nevertheless grace leaveth not the man, but it directeth and ordereth the forces of man and cherisheth the divine birth in the essence of the soul; . . . the spirit of man hath now passed over to the Godhead.

Being seated together in heavenly places in Christ Jesus does not mean lolling about on the mount of transfiguration, singing ecstatic hymns, and letting demon-possessed boys go to the devil in the valley; it means being in the accursed places of this earth as far as the walk of the feet is concerned, but in undisturbed communion with God.

In the historic Jesus Christ the spirit of man passed over to the Godhead and Jesus saw essentially, not experimentally, and the same thing happens when Christ is formed in us. God's grace does not leave a man after an experience of grace. The common idea of how to live the right life seems to be that it is by getting continual "bouts" of God's grace, that an insight into God's grace will last us several days. As a matter of fact it won't last us any time. That is not what God's grace means.

". . . while we look not at the things which are seen"—that battle never stops. The things that are seen are not the devil, but the pressing things, the things that distract; when Christ is formed in us and the essential vision comes through looking at the things which are not seen, we find that God makes other people shadows. If my saintly friends are images of God to me, I have much further to go, yet. God alone must be my Stay and Source and everything. That is the way the godly life is lived.

What is a godly life? A life like God in my bodily edition. Imitation is the great stumbling block to sanctification. Be yourself first, then go to your own funeral, and let God for ever after be All in all.

*The quotations are from the book entitled The Following of Christ, by John Tauler.*

# VII. THE PHILOSOPHY OF REASON

## Essence of Reason in the Saint

> *. . . being ready always to give answer to every man that asketh you a reason concerning the hope that is in you. (1 Peter 3:15 RV)*

To give an answer concerning the hope that is in us is not the same thing as convincing by reasonable argument why that hope is in us. A line we are continually apt to be caught by is that of argumentatively reasoning out why we are what we are; we cannot argue that out. There is not a saint amongst us who can give explicit reasonings concerning the hope that is in us, but we can always give this reason: we have received the Holy Spirit, and He has witnessed that the truths of Jesus are the truths for us. When we give that answer, anyone who hears it and refuses to try the same way of getting at the truth is condemned. If a man refuses one way of getting at the truth because he does not like that way, he ceases to be an honest man.

### (a) The Reach of Reason

> *I live; and yet no longer I, but Christ liveth in me. (Galatians 2:20 RV)*

> *The reason . . . is always striving after this essential working. . . . By this act of hastening after the divine work, she empties herself of all created images, and with a supernatural light she presseth into the mystery of the hidden Godhead.*

Reason always strives for a true expression. Soul is spirit expressing itself rationally, and whenever the work of God in a man's soul (as in the Apostle Paul's) is stated, it does not contradict the rational element, it transcends it. When a man is born again his personality becomes dead to earth as the source of its inspiration and is only alive to God. The great snare is to make reason work in the circle of our experience and not in the circle of God. As long as we use the image of our experience, of our feelings, of our answers to prayer, we shall never begin to understand what the Apostle Paul means when he says, "I live; and yet no longer I, but Christ liveth in me" (RV). The whole exercise of man's essential reason is drawing on God as the source of life. The hindrance comes when we begin to keep sensuous images spiritually in our minds. Those of us who have never had visions or ecstasies ought to be very thankful. Visions, and any emotions at all, are the greatest snare to a spiritual life, because immediately we get them we are apt to build them round our reasoning, and our reasoning round them and go no further. Over and over again sanctified people stagnate, they do not go back and they do not go on, they stagnate, they become stiller and stiller, and muddier and muddier, spiritually not morally, until ultimately there comes a sort of scum over the spiritual life and you wonder what is the matter with them. They are still true to God, still true to their testimony of what God has done for them, but they have never exercised the great God-given reason that is in them and got beyond the images of their experience into the knowledge that "God alone is life"—transcending all we call experience. It is because people will not take the labour to think that the snare gets hold of them, and remember, thinking is a tremendous labour (see 2 Corinthians 10:5).

### (b) The Reaction against Reason

> Be ye not as the horse, or as the mule, which have no understanding. (Psalm 32:9)

> For what the creature chooseth instead of God is done by sensuality and not by the reason . . . and whoso chooseth the creature instead of God, is not a rational man, but is as an irrational beast.

We use the term rational when we should say "sensual." Sensuality is a word that has lost its meaning in the higher realm to us, we only talk of sensuality on the grovelling line, but sensuality reaches higher, it means that bodily satisfaction is taken as the source of life—what I possess, what I feel, that is not rationalism but sensuality, and when it is allowed to dominate it works out as Paul says—they "became vain in their reasonings, and their senseless heart was darkened" (rv; see Romans 1:18-23). If we will let reason act it will make itself so felt that a man has to say, "There is more than this"; the visible things he sees and knows awaken in him a sense that there is something more than these. Reason must not be prevented from reaching to God.

In the religious domain sensuality takes another guise, it becomes either pietistic or ritualistic, both are irrational. The pietistic tendency in this country is a much bigger curse than the ritualistic tendency, that is a mere excrescence that will be always as long as human beings are. The real peril is the sensual piety that is not based on a rational life with God, but on certain kinds of devotion, certain needs of consecration, certain demands of my personal life. When you come to the New Testament, particularly the writings of the Apostle Paul, you find that kind of piety is torn to shreds (e.g. Colossians 2:20-23). All fanaticism and the things that are foreign to the teachings of Jesus Christ start from spiritual sensuality, which means I have images in my mind of what I want to be, and what I am, and what I have experienced. These images hinder reason from working. Beware of any image at all in your mind but Jesus Christ, an image of sanctification, or devotion, or any other thing on earth will be the peril of your rational spiritual life. Have we any idea that it is our devotion, our consecration, the times we give to prayer, the service rendered, what we have given up, because we have been through this and that experience we are where we are?—every one of them is a hidden irrational snare. No wonder the Apostle Paul was so anxious we should get on this rational line. The essence of reason in the saint—what is it? The Holy Ghost in me being obeyed, revealing the things of Jesus.

### (c) The Right Rational Man

> . . . but the water that I shall give him shall become in him a well of water. . . . I am the bread of life. (John 4:14 rv; 6:35)

> For the right reason seeketh God, and removes from creatures whether they be bodily or spiritual, and whoso cometh to this reason is a right, rational man, whose reason is shone through with divine light, in which you know the Godhead and forget the earthy.

let alone to anyone else. The reason for it is that God wants to get us out of the love of virtue and in love with the God of virtue—stripped of all possessions but our knowledge of Him.

### (b) The Most Extraordinary Wonder (2 Corinthians 9:6-15)

> And God is able to make all grace abound unto you. (2 Corinthians 9:8 RV)

> So long as a man hath he must give, and when he hath nothing more he is free. Freedom is much nobler than giving was before. for he giveth no more in accident but in essence.

Our Lord emptied Himself (RV) and had nothing all the days of His earthly life, consequently He was free for God to lavish His gifts through Him to others. Think of the rushes with which we come in front of our Heavenly Father; whenever we see an occasion we rush in and say, "I can do this, you need not trouble God." I wonder if we are learning determinedly to possess nothing? It is possessing things that makes us so conceited—"Oh yes, I can give prayer for you; I can give this and that for you." We have to get to the place about which Jesus talked to the rich young ruler where we are so absolutely empty and poor that we have nothing, and God knows we have nothing, then He can do through us what He likes. Would that we would quickly get rid of all we have, give it away till there is nothing left, then there is a chance for God to pour through in rivers for other people.

### (c) The More Exceeding Worship

> I beseech you therefore . . . to present your bodies a living sacrifice, . . . which is your spiritual worship [mg]. (Romans 12:1 RV)

> Therefore also a teacher saith, "It is good when a man imparts his property and cometh to the help of his fellow men; but it is far better to give all and to follow Christ in a poor life."

Worship is giving the best we have unreservedly to God. Jesus Christ was entirely merciful because He kept nothing at all. We are merciful in spots, in a fragmentary way, because we will stick to our opinionettes. Whatever makes us spiritually satisfied will twist our mercy at once, because an opinionette is attached to every spot where we are satisfied, and when anyone comes in contact with that spot of satisfaction we are merciless to them. Jesus Christ was never merciless, and it is only as we draw on His life that we are like our Father in heaven. The only safety is to live the life hid with Christ in God. As long as we are consciously there, we are not there. It is only when we are there that it never occurs to us that we are, but the evidence is strong because others are getting the blessings of God through us and are helping themselves to us, even as Jesus Christ was made broken bread and poured-out wine for us. God cannot make some of us into broken bread because there are bits of unbaked dough in us that would produce indigestion. We have to go into the furnace again to be baked properly until we are no more like Ephraim, "a cake not turned."

## Expression of Resurrection Reason in the Saint

> Blessed are the dead which die in the Lord.
> (Revelation 14:13)

### (a) The Matter of Death

> Except a grain of wheat fall into the earth and die, it abideth by itself alone; but if it die, it beareth much fruit. (John 12:24 RV)

> Therefore we should make ourselves poor, that we may fundamentally die, and in this dying be made alive again.

Death is God's delightful way of giving us life. The monks in the early ages shut themselves away from everything to prove they were dead to it all, and when they got away they found themselves more alive than ever. Jesus never shut Himself away from things, the first place He took His disciples to was a marriage feast. He did not cut Himself off from society, He was not aloof, so much was He not aloof that they called Him "a gluttonous man, and a winebibber!" But there was one characteristic of Jesus—He was fundamentally dead to the whole thing, it had no appeal to Him. The "hundredfold" which Jesus promised means that God can trust a man anywhere and with anything when he is fundamentally dead to things.

### (b) The Manner of Devotion

> *If thou wouldest be perfect, go, sell that thou hast, . . . and come, follow Me. (Matthew 19:21 RV)*
>
> *This selling means the self-denial of man; the giving away is virtue, the following of Jesus is fundamentally to die, so that dying completely to himself God may live perfectly in him.*

Immediately that is experienced we are alive with the effulgent life of God. We use the phrase "drawing on the resurrection life of Jesus," but try it, you cannot draw on it when you like. You will never get one breath of that life until you are dead, that is, dead to any desire that you want a blessing for body or soul or spirit. Immediately you die to that, the life of God is in you, and you don't know where you are with the exuberance of it. To put it in the negative way—the bits in us that won't yield to God are the bits we cling to. We are always going back to the grave and saying, "I was always respectable here; I don't need Christ there; I always had a good view of what was right and pure." Instantly the life of God in us wilts; but when the dying is gone through with and maintained (I am not talking about dying to sin, but about dying right out to my right to myself in any shape or form), then the life of Jesus can be manifested in my mortal flesh (see 2 Corinthians 4:10-12).

### (c) The Method of the Discipline of Death

> *For ye died, and your life is hid with Christ in God. (Colossians 3:3 RV)*
>
> *Blessed is the man who can die all manner of deaths, but this dying is of such a nature that no man can rightly understand it, and he is the most rational who understandeth this dying*

*the best. For no one understandeth it save he to whom God hath revealed it.*

This secret is revealed to the humblest child of God who receives, recognises and relies on the Holy Spirit, and it leads to only one place, the effulgent life of God, while we walk in the light as He is in the light. The trouble with most of us is that we will walk only in the light of our conviction of what the light is. If you are live to God He will never take from you the amazing mercy of having something put to death. Jesus sacrificed His natural life and made it spiritual by obeying His Father's voice, and we have any number of glorious opportunities of proving how much we love God by the delighted way we go to sacrifice for Him.

*The quotations are from the book entitled The Following of Christ, by John Tauler.*

# VIII. The Philosophy of Love

*Mark 12:29-31*

## The Way of the Sovereign Preference of the Heart

*Lovest thou Me? (John 21:15-17)*

*And these are the right lovers of God, who love God with
their whole heart. And they who love God with their whole
heart give up all bodily things for the sake of God.*

Faith, hope, love (RV), the three supernatural virtues, have a
two-fold aspect in the saint's life. The first is seen in the early
experiences of grace when these virtues are accidental; the second,
when grace is worked into us and these virtues are essential and
abiding. When the work of God's grace begins, "the love of God is
shed abroad in our hearts by the Holy Ghost," not the power to
love God, but the essential nature of God. When we experience
what technically we call being born again of the Spirit of God, we
have "spurts" of faith, hope, love, they come but we cannot grip
them and they go; when we experience what technically we call
sanctification those virtues abide, they are not accidental any more.
The test of the life "hid with Christ in God" is not the experience
of salvation or sanctification, but the relationship into which those
experiences have led us. It is only by realising the love of God in us
by His grace that we are led by His entrancing power in us whither
we would not.

Love is the sovereign preference of my person for another
person, and Jesus says that other Person must be Himself. Ask
yourself what sort of conception you have of loving God. The
majority of us have a bloodless idea, an impersonal, ethereal, vague
abstraction, called "love to God." Read Jesus Christ's conception;
He mentions relationships of the closest, most personal, most
passionate order, and says that our love for Him must be closer and
more personal than any of those (see Luke 14:26). How is it to be?
Only by the work of the sovereign grace of God. If we have not
realised the shedding abroad of the essential nature of God in our
hearts, the words of Jesus ought to make us realise the necessity of

it—"Thou shalt love the Lord thy God from [rv mg] all thy heart.
. . ." To love God with all my heart means to be weaned from the
dominance of earthly things as a guide; there is only one dominant
passion in the deepest centre of the personality, and that is the love
of God.

## The Way of the Soul's Passion for God

> *Whosoever shall lose his life for My sake shall find*
> *it. (Matthew 16:25 RV)*

> *They also love with their whole soul; that is, when they give*
> *up their life for the sake of God; for the soul giveth life to the*
> *body, and this same life they give entirely to God.*

The only way to love God with all our soul is to give up our
lives for His sake, not give our lives to God, that is an elemental
point, but when that has been done, after our lives have been given
to God, we ought to lay them down for God (see 1 John 3:16).
Jesus Christ laid down His holy life for His Father's purposes, then
if we are God's children we have to lay down our lives for His sake,
not for the sake of a truth, not for the sake of devotion to a doctrine,
but for Jesus Christ's sake—the personal relationship all through
(cf. Luke 6:22-23). Have I ever realised the glorious opportunity I
have of laying down my life for Jesus? It does not mean that we lay
down our lives in the crisis of death; what God wants is the sacrifice
*through* death, which enables us to do what Jesus did—He
sacrificed His life; His death comes in as a totally new revelation.
Every morning we wake, and every moment of the day, we have
this glorious privilege of sacrificing our holy selves to and for Jesus
Christ (see Romans 12:1).

Beware of the subtle danger that gets hold of our spiritual life
when we trust in our experience. Experience is absolutely nothing
if it is not the gateway only to a relationship. The experience of
sanctification is not the slightest atom of use unless it has enabled
me to realise that that experience means a totally new relationship.
Sanctification may take a few moments of realised transaction, but
all the rest of the life goes to prove what that transaction means.

## The Way of the Mind's Penetration into God (1 John 3:2-3)

> *. . . when He shall appear, we shall be like Him. (1 John 3:2)*

> *They also love God with all their mind; that is, when their mind soareth above all created things, and penetrates into the uncreated good, which is God, and then loseth itself in the secret darkness of the unknown God. Therein it loseth itself and escapeth, so that it can no more come out.*

To love God with all our mind we have to "soar above created things, and penetrate into the uncreated good," viz. God. When the Spirit of God begins to deal on this side of things we shall feel at sea, if we are not spiritual, as to what is meant; when we are spiritual we feel with our hearts, not with our heads—"Yes, I begin to see what it means." When anything begins to get vague, bring yourself up against the revelation of Jesus Christ, He is a Fact, and He is the Pattern of what we ought to be as Christians (cf. Matthew 5:48). How much of our time are we giving for God to graduate us in the essential life? We know all about the accidental life, about the sudden spurts that come to us, the sudden times of illumination and sweet inspiration from God's Book; what Our Lord is getting at is not a life of that description at all, but a life that has lost all sense of its own isolation and smallness and is taken up with God. Not only is the life hid with Christ in God, but the heart is blazing with love to God, and the mind is able to begin slowly bit by bit to bring every thought into captivity to the obedience of Christ, till we never trouble about ourselves or our conscious life, we are taken up only with thoughts that are worthy of God.

## The Way of the Strength of Stillness for God (Ephesians 3:16-19)

> *That He would grant you . . . to be strengthened with might . . . ; that Christ may dwell in your hearts by faith . . . (Ephesians 3:16-17)*

*They further love God with all their strength; that is, they ordain all their powers according to the highest discretion, and they direct all of them to one end, and with this effort they penetrate into God.*

The whole strength of the personal life, the personal spirit, is to be so gripped by the Spirit of God that we begin to comprehend His meaning. It is always risky to use a phrase with a fringe, a phrase that has a definite kernel of meaning but a fringe of something that is not definite. The way we get off on to the fringe is by ecstasy, and ecstasies may mean anything from the devil to God. An ecstasy is something which takes us clean beyond our own control and we do not know what we are doing, whether we are being inspired by God or the devil, whether we are jabbering with angels' tongues or demons'. When you come to the words of Our Lord or of the Apostle Paul the one great safeguard is the absolute sanity of the whole thing. ". . . that ye . . . may be able to comprehend . . . and to know"—there is no ecstasy there, no being carried out of yourself into a swoon, no danger of what the mystics of the Middle Ages called Quietism, no danger of losing the conditions of morality; but slowly and surely we begin to comprehend the love of Christ, i.e., the essential nature of God which the Holy Ghost has imparted to us, which enables us to live the same kind of life that Jesus lived down here through His marvellous Atonement. Anything that partakes of the nature of swamping our personality out of our control is never of God. Do we ever find a time in the life of the Lord Jesus Christ when He was carried beyond His own control? Never once. Do we ever find Him in a spiritual panic, crediting God with it? Never once; and the one great marvel of the work of the Holy Ghost is that the sanity of Jesus Christ is stamped on every bit of it. Jesus said we should know the work of the Holy Ghost by these signs—"He shall glorify Me"; "He shall teach you all things, and bring to your remembrance all that I said unto you" (RV), and, "He will guide you into all truth." The Spirit of God does not dazzle and startle and amaze us into worshipping God; that is why He takes such a long while, it is bit by bit, process by process, with every power slowly realising and comprehending "with all saints. . . ." We cannot comprehend it alone; the "together" aspect of the New Testament is wonderful. Beware of all those things that run off on a tangent spiritually. They begin by saying, "God gave me an impulse to do this"; God never gave anyone any impulse. Watch Jesus Christ, the first thing He checked in the training of the twelve was impulse. Impulse may be all right morally and physically, but it is never right spiritually. Wherever spiritual impulse has been allowed to have its way it has led the soul astray. We must check all impulses by this test—Does this glorify Jesus, or does it only glorify ourselves? Does it bring to our remembrance something Jesus said, that is, does it connect itself with the word of God, or is it beginning to turn us aside and make us seek great things for ourselves? That is where the snare comes. Nowadays, people seem to have an idea that these ecstatic, visionary, excitable, lunatic moments glorify God; they do not, they give an opportunity to the devil. The one thing Jesus Christ did when He came in contact with lunacy was to heal it, and the greatest work of the devil is that he is producing lunacy in the name of God all over the world in the spiritual realm, making people who did know God go off on tangents. What did Jesus say? ". . . so as to lead astray, if possible, even the elect" (RV). Beware of being carried off into any kind of spiritual ecstasy either in private or in public. There is nothing about ecstasy in these verses: "Thou shalt love the Lord thy God with all thy heart"—the sovereign preference of our personality for God. Can I say before God, "For in all the world there is none but Thee, my God, there is none but Thee"? Is it true? is there a woman there? is there a man there? is there a child there? is there a friend there? "Thou shalt love the Lord thy God with all thy heart." Do you say, "But that is so stern"? The reason it is stern is that when once God's mighty grace gets my heart wholly absorbed in Him, every other love of my life is safe; but if my love to God is not dominant, my love may prove to be lust. Nearly all the cruelty in the world springs from not understanding this. Lust in its highest and lowest form simply means I seek for a creature to give me what God alone can give, and I become cruel and vindictive and jealous and spiteful to the one from whom I demand what God alone can give.

". . . and with all thy soul." What are we laying down our lives for? Why do so many Christians go a-slumming? why do so many go to the foreign field? why do so many seek for the salvation of souls? Let us haul ourselves up short and measure ourselves by the standard of Jesus Christ. He said, "The Son of man is come to seek and to save that which was lost." The mainspring of His love for human souls was His love to the Father; then if I go a-slumming for the same reason, I can never do too much of it; but if my desire for the salvation of souls is the evangelical commercial craze, may God blast it out of me by the fire of the Holy Ghost. There is such a thing as commercialism in souls as there is in business. When we testify and speak, why do we?: is it out of the accident of a poor little paltry experience that we have had, or is it because the whole life is blazing with an amazing desire, planted there by the Holy Ghost, for God to glorify Himself?

> *Arrived here, all the powers keep silence and rest; this also is the highest work that the powers can perform, when they are inactive and let God only work.*

It is only when our lives are hid with Christ in Godthat we learn how to be silent unto God, not silent about Him, but silent with the strong restful certainty that all is well, behind everything stands God, and the strength of the soul is that it knows it. There are no panics intellectual or moral. What a lot of panicky sparrows we are, the majority of us. We chatter and tweet under God's eaves until we cannot hear His voice at all—until we learn the wonderful life and music of the Lord Jesus telling us that our heavenly Father is the God of the sparrows, and by the marvellous transformation of grace He can turn the sparrows into His nightingales that can sing through every night of sorrow. A sparrow cannot sing through a night of sorrow, and no soul can sing through a night of sorrow unless it has learned to be silent unto God—one look, one thought about my Father in heaven, and it is all right.

## The Way of the Freedom of the Will (Romans 6:21-22)

> *But now being made free from sin . . . (Romans 6:22)*

> *. . . Thus is the mind bound by God. To this it might be said, If this is so, the freedom of the will is taken away. I answer, the freedom of the will is not taken away but given to it, for then is the will quite free when it cannot bear anything save what God willeth.*

"Thus is the mind bound by God. . . ." The complaint of a person who is not spiritual when one talks like that, is that a man's free will is destroyed. It is not, it is given to him. The only thing that gives a personality freedom of will is the salvation of Jesus Christ. The will is not a faculty, will is the whole man active—body, soul and spirit. Let a man get right with God through the Atonement and his activity becomes in that manner and measure akin to Jesus Christ. The whole of my will free to do God's will, that means a holy scorn of putting my neck under any yoke but the yoke of the Lord Jesus Christ. Where are Christians putting their necks nowadays? Why, nine out of every nine and a half of us are absolute cowards, we will only put our necks under the yoke of the set we belong to. It means—"without the camp, bearing His reproach." (See John 14:15; 15:9-10)

## The Way of Hearing the Eternal Word

> *If a man love Me, he will keep My words. (John 14:23)*

> *When now man . . . cometh to the third degree of perfection, in which he heareth, in a silent, secret speaking, the everlasting Word which God the Father speaketh in the ground of souls . . .*

We all know how certain verses jump out of a page of the Bible and grip us, full of infinite sweetness and inspiration; at other times they do not. That is what people mean when they say God gave them a message—by the way, do not say that unless God does, we use phrases much too glibly. God may give you the kind of message He gave Isaiah, a blistering, burning message of the altar of God. To be able to hear "the silent, secret speaking" of the Father's voice in the words of the Bible is the essential groundwork of the soul of every saint.

"The words that I have spoken unto you are spirit, and are life" (John 6:63 RV). God makes His own word re-speak in us by His Spirit. He safeguarded that; He uses the words His Son used, and the words those used who He determined should write them (see 2 Peter 1:21). The great insubordination of to-day is, "Who are the apostles? God spake through them, why can't He speak through me?" He will not unless we let the Spirit of God interpret to us what those men said, then He will talk through us, but in no other way. When once a man has learned to hear with the inner ear the word of God he "discardeth his self-hood," and the natural delight in God's word is lost in the realisation that it is God Who is speaking. Do you want to know how self-hood works out?—"I have such a fine message, it will do for such and such an audience"; "I have got a wonderful exposition of this text." Well, burn it and never think any more about it. Give the best you have every time and everywhere. Learn to get into the quiet place where you can hear God's voice speak through the words of the Bible, and never be afraid that you will run dry, He will simply pour the word until you have no room to contain it. It won't be a question of hunting for messages or texts, but of opening the mouth wide and He fills it.

The outcome of Mark 12:29-31 is God four times over—God the King of my heart, God the King of my soul, God the King of my mind, God the King of my strength; nothing other than God; and the working out of it is that we show the same love to our fellow-men as God has shown us. That is the external aspect of this internal relationship, the sovereign preference of my person for God. The love of the heart for Jesus, the life laid down for Jesus, the mind thinking only for Jesus, the strength given over to Jesus, the will working only the will of God, and the ear of the personality hearing only what God has to say.

*The quotations are from the book entitled The Following of Christ, by John Tauler.*

# IX. THE PHILOSOPHY OF SACRIFICING

## Matthew 16:24-26

### *"I Wonder if I Will or if I Won't"*

God does not take the wilful "won't" out of us by salvation; at any stage we may say, "No, thank you, I am delighted to be saved and sanctified, but I am not going any further." Our Lord always prefaced His talks about discipleship with an "if"; it has no reference whatever to a soul's salvation or condemnation, but to the discipleship of the personality.

We must bear in mind that Our Lord in His teaching reveals unalterable and eternal principles. In Matthew 16:25 —"For whosoever would save his life shall lose it: and whosoever shall for My sake shall find it" (RV)—Jesus says that the eternal principle of human life is that something must be sacrificed; if we won't sacrifice the natural life, we do the spiritual. Our Lord is not speaking of a punishment to be meted out, He is revealing what is God's eternal principle at the back of human life. We may rage and fret, as men have done, against God's just principles, or we may submit and accept and go on; but Jesus reveals that these principles are as unalterable as God Himself.

"I wonder if I will or if I won't." In sanctification the freedom of the will is brought to its highest critical point. A good many people in order to express the marvellous emancipation that comes by God's salvation make the statement, "I cannot now do the things that are wrong." It is only then we have the choice; when Jesus Christ emancipates us from the power of sin, that second we have the power to disobey, before we had not the power, we were almost obliged to disobey because of the tendency in that direction. So this principle in its full meaning, "I wonder if I will or if I won't," works on the threshold of sanctification—"I wonder if I will devote myself to Jesus Christ, or to a doctrine, or a point of view of my own." Jesus says if we are to be His disciples we must sacrifice everything to that one thing.

## Innocent Light under Identification

*Take My yoke upon you, and learn of Me, . . . and
ye shall find rest unto your souls. (Matthew 11:29)*

*But what use doth it bring if a man alway dieth? It bringeth
a fivefold use. First, man draweth nigh thereby to his first
innocence. . . . They are best in this who have most died to
themselves for in that death and denial of self a new delight
springeth up, for the death that man suffereth thereby openeth
up the hidden joy. Christ also said, "Take My yoke upon
you—that is, My Passion—and ye will find rest unto your
souls."*

The only place we shall find rest is in the direct education by
Jesus in His Cross. A new delight springs up in any saint who
suffers the yoke of Christ. Beware of dissipating that yoke and
making it mean the yoke of a martyr. It is the yoke of a person who
owes all he has to the Cross of Christ. Paul wore the yoke when he
said, "For I determined not to know any thing among you, save
Jesus Christ, and Him crucified." "Take My yoke upon you"—it is
the one yoke men will not wear.

Have I taken the yoke of Christ upon me, and am I walking in
the innocent light that comes only from the Spirit of God through
the Atonement? When we are born again of the Spirit of God we
are made totally new creatures on the inside; that means we have to
live according to the new life of innocence that God has given us,
and not be dictated to by the clamouring defects of the temple into
which that life has been put. The danger is to become wise and
prudent, cumbered with much serving, and these things choke the
life God has put in (cf. Mark 4:19).

## Implicit Love under Identification

*Who shall separate us from the love of Christ?
(Romans 8:35)*

*The second use is, that in each such dying a new life ariseth
to man, and with this life every time a new love, so that man
is overflooded with grace, and his reason is enlightened with*

*divine light, his will is glowing with the fire of divine love . . .*
*so that no one can any more separate him from God.*

The natural life of a saint is neither pure nor impure; it is not pure necessarily because the heart is pure, it has to be made pure by the will of the person. To delight in sacrificing the natural to the spiritual means to be overflowing with the grace and love of God, and the manner and measure of the sacrificing depends on—"I wonder if I will or if I won't." Never say, if you are a thoughtful saint, "Since I have been sanctified I have done what I liked." If you have, you are immoral in that degree. If it were true, it would be true of the holiest Being Who ever lived, but it is said of Him that "even Christ pleased not Himself" (Romans 15:3; cf. John 8:28; Hebrews 5:8). There must be something to sacrifice. Jesus says, "If you would be My disciple, you must sacrifice the natural life," i.e., the life that is moral and right and good from the ordinary standpoint of man. We cannot use the terms of natural virtue in describing Jesus Christ. If you say that Jesus was a holy man you feel at once it is not sufficient; or take the terms of intense saintliness, you can never fit them on to Jesus Christ, because there is an element of fanaticism in every saint that there never was in the Lord. There is an amazing sanity in Jesus Christ that shakes the foundations of death and hell, no panic, absolute dominant mastery over everything—such a stupendous mastery that He let men take His strength from Him: "He was crucified through weakness," that was the acme of Godlike strength.

## Identity of Liberty under Identification

*Verily, verily, I say unto thee, except a man be born again, he cannot see the kingdom of God. (John 3:3)*

*Thirdly, if a man is quite pure he is emptied of all defective accident, and receptive of God alone. God is present in all things; if you accomplish all things so, then God only remaineth to us; but this purity must be sought by dying, and if the soul is freed from everything else, she is in a condition to bring forth the Son of God within her.*

Bear in mind the audience of Jesus when He said these words; Jesus said them to a mature, upright, godly man, there is no mention of sin, that will come in due course, it comes in the order Jesus said it would, by the Holy Spirit (see John 16:8-9). When the Son of God is born in us He brings us into the liberty of God. "Whosoever is begotten of God doeth no sin" (RV). The only way we can be born again is by renouncing all other good. The "old man," or the man of old, means all the things which have nothing to do with the new life. It does not mean sins, any coward among us will give up wrong things, but will he give up right things? Will we give up the virtues, the principles, the recognition of things that are dearer to the "Adam" life than the God life? The nature of the "Adam" disposition in us rebels against sacrificing natural good. Jesus says, "If you don't sacrifice natural good, you will barter the life I represent." This is the thing men resent with what Paul calls "enmity" (Romans 8:7). The preachers and teachers who have not taken on them the yoke of Christ are always inclined to exalt natural good, natural virtues, natural nobility and heroism; the consequence is Jesus Christ pales more and more into the background until He becomes "as a root out of a dry ground." Imagine a pagan who worshipped natural virtues being told that the Nazarene Carpenter was God's idea expressed in His last syllable to this order of things—it would be, as Paul said, "foolishness unto him." The same thing persists to-day.

## Infusion of Likeness under Identification

> *If we walk in the light, as He is in the light . . . (1 John 1:7)*

> The fourth use ariseth if God is born in the soul, when God ravisheth the spirit from the soul and casteth her into the darkness of His Godhead, so that she becometh quite like unto God . . . so that the man becometh a son of grace, as he is a son of nature.

To be a son of God is to be free from the tyranny of the show of things. Adam preferred to take the show of things for the substance, that is, he preferred not to see that the "garment" was not the Person; he refused to listen to the voice of the Creator behind the garment, and when the Creator moved quickly, all Adam could do was to hang on to the skirts of the garment, clutch at the show of things, and the human race has been doing it ever since. Exactly what Jesus said, the spiritual has been bartered because we preferred the natural. The natural is only a manifestation of what is behind. If we walk in the light, not as holy men are in the light, but as God is in the light, we see behind the show of things—God. We become the sons of God by a regenerating internal birth, and when that regenerating principle inside takes its marvellous sway over the natural on the outside, the two are transformed into exactly what God intended them to be. That is the full meaning of the Redemption, but in order to get there the natural must be sacrificed. If I prefer to hug my Father's skirt, I must not be surprised at finding myself in darkness when He gives it a sudden pull; but if I let my Father take me up in His arms, then He can move His skirts as He likes—"Therefore will we not fear, though the earth do change, and though the mountains be moved in the heart of the seas" (RV). I am no longer caught up in the show of things. The saints who are alive when Jesus comes will be "changed, in a moment, in the twinkling of an eye"; all the show of things will be changed instantly by the touch of God into reality.

## Incorporation of Life under Identification

> For as many as are led by the Spirit of God, these are sons of God. (Romans 8:14 rv; cf. Philippians 2:15)

> Fifthly, if the soul be raised into God, it reigneth also with God. . . . Thus the spirit can do all things with God; he commandeth all with God, he ordereth and leadeth all with God; what God omits, he omitteth; what God doeth, he doeth with God; he worketh all things with God. This unspeakable perfection we obtain through dying.

Being born again of the Spirit is not contrary to God's original plan; for a time it has to be apparently contrary to it because Adam refused to sacrifice the life of nature to the will of God and transform it into a spiritual life by obeying the voice of God. The natural has to be sacrificed for a time, but we shall find the Redemption of Jesus works out *via* the natural in the end—"And I saw a new heaven *and a new earth.*" In the meantime to be a disciple of Jesus means to be "taboo" in this order of things.

Remember, it was not the "offscouring" that crucified Jesus, it was the highest reach of natural morality crucified Him. It is the refined, cultured, religious, moral people who refuse to sacrifice the natural for the spiritual. When once you get that thought, you understand the inveterate detestation of the Cross of Christ. Where are we with regard to this barter? Are we disciples of Jesus? Who is first, or what is first, in our lives? who is the dominating personality that is dearer to us than life, ourselves or someone else? If it is someone else, who is it? It is only on such lines as these that we come to understand what Jesus meant when He said, "If any man would come after Me, let him deny himself" (RV). What He means is that He and what He stands for must be first. The enemies of the Cross of Christ, whom Paul characterises so strongly, and does it weeping, are those who represent the type of things that attract far more than Jesus Christ. Never put a false issue before men or before yourself. We begin to compare ourselves with ourselves—"Oh well, I have always had refined susceptibilities; I have always had an admiration for what is noble and true and good"; Jesus says, Die to it all. Read Philippians 3—"What things were gain to me, these have I counted loss for Christ" (RV).

"Then said Jesus unto His disciples, If any man would come after Me, let him . . . follow Me." The first "Follow Me" was a fascination for natural ideals. "Are ye able to drink the cup that I drink? . . . We are able" (RV). There is no arrogance there, only hopeless misunderstanding. We all say, "Yes, Lord, I will do anything"; but will you go to the death of that—the death of being willing to go to the death for the noble and true and right? Will you let Jesus take the sense of the heroic right out of you? will you let Him make you see yourself as He sees you until for one moment you stand before the Cross and say, "Nothing in my hands I bring"?

How many of us are there to-day? Talk about getting people to hear that, they won't have it! Jesus says they won't. No crowd on earth will ever listen to that, and if under some pretence you get them and preach the Cross of Christ they will turn with a snubbing offence from the whole thing as they did in Our Lord's day (John 6:60, 66). The abominable "show business" is creeping into the very ranks of the saved and sanctified—"We must get the crowds." We must not; we must keep true to the Cross; let folks come and go as they will, let movements come and go, let ourselves be swept along or not, the one main thing is—true to the yoke of Christ, His Cross. The one thing we have to stand against is what is stated in Hebrews 12:1, "Therefore let us . . . lay aside every encumbrance [mg] and the sin which doth so easily beset us" (RV), the sin which is admired (rv mg) in many—the sin that gathers round your feet and stops you running; get stripped of the whole thing and run, with your eye on your File Leader, making "straight paths for your feet, that that which is lame be not turned out of the way" (RV).

*The quotations are from the book entitled The Following of Christ, by John Tauler.*

# X. The Philosophy of Discipleship

*Let no man think that sudden in a minute*
*All is accomplished and the work is done:—*
*Though with thine earliest dawn thou shouldst begin it*
*Scarce were it ended in thy setting sun.*

Discipleship must always be a personal matter; we can never become disciples in crowds, or even in twos. It is so easy to talk about what "we" mean to do—"we" are going to do marvellous things, and it ends in none of us doing anything. The great element of discipleship is the personal one.

The disciples in the days of His flesh were in a relationship to our Lord which we cannot imagine; they had a unique relationship which no other men have had or will have. We may use the relationship of these men to Jesus as illustrative of those who are devoted to Him but not yet born from above (RV MG), or we may take them as pointing out lines of discipleship after the work of grace has been begun. Discipleship may be looked at from many aspects because it is not a dogma but a declaration. We are using discipleship in this study as an illustration of what happens after salvation. Salvation and discipleship are not one and the same thing. Whenever our Lord speaks of discipleship He prefaces what He says with an "IF." "If any man come after Me . . ." Discipleship is based on devotion to Jesus Christ, not on adherence to a doctrine.

## Potential Position by Grace

*Then answered Peter and said unto Him, Lo, we*
*have left all, and followed Thee; what then shall we*
*have? (Matthew 19:27 rv; cf. 15:24)*

Potential means existing in possibility, not in reality. By regeneration in its twofold phase of salvation and sanctification we are potentially able to perform all the will of God. That does not mean we are doing it, it means that we can do it if we will because God has empowered us (see Philippians 2:12-13). A man in whom the grace of God has begun its work—the grace of God does not respect persons, so I mean any kind of man you can think of—is potentially in the sight of God as Christ: the possibility of being as Christ is there. Whenever the grace of God strikes a man's consciousness and he begins to realise what he is in God's sight, he becomes fanatical, if he is healthy. We have to make allowance in ourselves and others for "the swing of the pendulum," which makes us go to the opposite extreme of what we were before. When once the grace of God has touched our hearts we see nothing but God, we do not see Him in relation to anything else, but only in relation to ourselves on the inside, and we forget to open the gate for gladness. Fanaticism is the insane sign of a sane relationship to God in its initial working. The joy of the incoming grace of God always makes us fanatical. It is the potential position by grace, and God leaves us in that nursery of bliss just as long as He thinks fit, then He begins to take us on another step; we have to make that possible relationship actual. We have not only to be right with God inside, we have to be manifestly rightly related to God on the outside, and this brings us to the painful matter of discipline.

## Practical Path in Grace

> *And Jesus said unto them, Verily I say unto you, that ye which have followed Me, in the regeneration when the Son of man shall sit on the throne of His glory, ye also shall sit upon twelve thrones. (Matthew 19:28 rv; cf. Matthew 10:38)*

> To abandon all, to strip one's self of all, in order to seek and follow Jesus Christ naked to Bethlehem, where He was born, naked to the hall where He was scourged, and naked to Calvary where He died on the cross, is so great a mystery that neither the thing, nor the knowledge of it, is given to any but through faith in the Son of God.
>
> John Wesley

The practical path in grace is to make what is possible actual. That is where many of us hang back; we say, "No, I prefer the bliss and the delight of the simple, ignorant babyhood of 'Bethlehem,' I like to be carried in the arms of God; I do not want to transform that innocence into holy character." The following in the steps of Jesus in discipleship is so great a mystery that few enter into it. When once the Face of the Lord Jesus Christ has broken through, all ecstasies and experiences dwindle in His presence, and the one dominant Leadership becomes more and more clear. We have seen Jesus as we never saw Him before, and the impulsion in us by the grace of God is that we must follow in His steps. As in the life of Mary, the mother of our Lord, a sword pierced through her own soul because of the Son of God, so the sword pierces our natural life as we sacrifice it to the will of God and thus make it spiritual. That is the first lesson in the practical path of grace. We go through bit by bit and realise that there are things Jesus says and the Holy Spirit applies to us, at which the natural cries out, "That is too hard."

## The Practice of Pain in Grace

> And every one that hath left houses . . . for My name's sake, shall receive a hundredfold. (Matthew 19:29 rv; cf. Luke 14:26-27)

"If any man come to Me, and hate not . . . , he cannot be My disciple." The word "hate" sounds harsh, and yet it is uttered by the most human of human beings because Jesus was Divine; there was never a human breast that beat with more tenderness than Jesus Christ's. The word "hate" is used as a vehement protest against the pleas to which human nature is only too ready to give a hearing. If we judge our Lord by a standard of humanity that does not recognise God, we have to put a black mark against certain things He said. One such mark would come in connection with His words to His mother at Cana, "Woman, what have I to do with thee?" Another would come in connection with John the Baptist; instead of Jesus going and taking His forerunner out of prison, He simply sends a message to him through his disciples—"Go your way, and tell John. . . . And blessed is he, whosoever shall not be offended in Me." But if we could picture the look of our Lord when He spoke the words, it would make a great difference to the interpretation.

There was no being on earth with more tenderness than the Lord Jesus, no one who understood the love of a mother as He did, and if we read this into His attitude towards His mother and towards John we shall find the element of pain to which He continually alludes, that is, we have to do things that hurt the best relationships in life without any explanation. If we make our Lord's words the reply of a callous nature, we credit Him with the spirit of the devil; but interpret them in the light of what Jesus says about discipleship, and we shall see that we must sacrifice the natural in order to transform it into the spiritual. All through our Lord's teaching that comes—"If you are going to be My disciple, you must barter the natural." Our Lord is not talking about sin, but about the natural life which is neither moral nor immoral; we make it moral or immoral. Over and over again we come to the practice of pain in grace, and it is the only explanation of the many difficult things Jesus said which make people rebel, or else say that He did not say them.

Have we begun to walk the practical path in grace? Do we know anything about the practice of pain? Watch what the Bible has to say about suffering, and you will find the great characteristic of the life of a child of God is the power to suffer, and through that suffering the natural is transformed into the spiritual. The thing we kick against most is the question of pain and suffering. We have naturally the idea that if we are happy and peaceful we are all right. "I came not to send peace, but a sword," said our Lord—a striking utterance from the Prince of Peace. Happiness is not a sign that we are right with God; happiness is a sign of satisfaction, that is all, and the majority of us can be satisfied on too low a level. Jesus Christ disturbs every kind of satisfaction that is less than delight in God. Every strand of sentimental satisfaction is an indication of how much farther we have to go before we understand the life of God, it is the satisfaction of a smug self-interest which God by circumstances and pain shocks out of us as we go in the discipline of life.

### Protest of Power through Grace

*. . . ye also shall sit upon twelve thrones. (Matthew 19:28)*

Physical power is nothing before moral power. A frail simple girl can overcome a brute who has the strength of an ox by moral superiority. Think of our Lord's life. The New Testament does not refer to the scene in the Garden as a miracle—"when therefore He said unto them, I am He, they went backward, and fell to the ground" (RV)—it was the inevitable protest of power of a pure holy Being facing unholy men from whom all power went. The wonder is not that Jesus showed His marvellous power, but that He did not show it. He continually covered it up.

> *Oh! wonderful the wonders left undone!—*
> *And scarce less wonderful than those He wrought!*
> *Oh, self-restraint, passing all human thought,*
> *To have all power and be—as having none!*

The great marvel of Jesus was that He was voluntarily weak. "He was crucified through weakness," and, says Paul, "we also are weak in Him." Any coward amongst us can hit back when hit, but it takes an exceedingly strong nature not to hit back. Jesus Christ never did. "Who, when He was reviled, reviled not again; when He suffered, He threatened not"; and if we are going to follow His example we shall find that all His teaching leads along that line. But ultimately, at the final wind-up of His great purpose, those who have followed His steps reign with Him. Those who reign with Him are not the sanctified in possibility, in ecstasy, but those who have gone through actually. Equal duties, not equal rights, is the keynote of the spiritual world; equal rights is the clamour of the natural world. The protest of power through grace, if we are following Jesus, is that we no longer insist on our rights, we see that we fulfil our duty.

That is the philosophy of a poor, perfect, pure discipleship. Remember, these are not conditions of salvation, but of discipleship. Those of us who have entered into a conscious experience of the salvation of Jesus by the grace of God, whose whole inner life is drawn towards God, have the privilege of being disciples, if we will. The Bible never refers to degrees of salvation, but there are degrees of it in actual experience. The spiritual privileges and opportunities of all disciples are equal; it has nothing to do with education or natural ability. "One is your Master, even Christ." We have no business to bring in that abomination of the lower regions that makes us think too little of ourselves; to think too little of ourselves is simply the obverse side of conceit. If I am a disciple of Jesus, He is my Master, I am looking to Him, and the thought of self never enters. So crush on the threshold of your mind any of those lame, limping "oh I can'ts, you see I am not gifted." The great stumbling block in the way of some people being simple disciples is that they are gifted, so gifted that they won't trust God. So clear away all those things from the thought of discipleship; we all have absolutely equal privileges, and there is no limit to what God can do in and through us.

Jesus Christ never allows anywhere any room for the disciple to say, "Now, Lord, I am going to serve Thee." It never once comes into His outlook on discipleship that the disciple works for Him. He said, "As the Father hath sent Me, even so send I you" (RV). How did the Father send Jesus? To do His will. How does Jesus send His disciples? To do His will. "Ye shall be My witnesses" (RV)—a satisfaction to Me wherever you are placed. Our Lord's conception of discipleship is not that we work for God, but that God works through us; He uses us as He likes; He allots our work where He chooses, and we learn obedience as our Master did (Hebrews 5:8).

The one test of a teacher sent from God is that those who listen see and know Jesus Christ better than ever they did. If you are a teacher sent from God your worth in God's sight is estimated by the way you enable people to see Jesus. How are you going to tell whether I am a teacher sent from God or not? You can tell it in no other way than this—that you know Jesus Christ better than ever you did. If a teacher fascinates with his doctrine, his teaching never came from God. The teacher sent from God is the one who clears the way to Jesus and keeps it clear; souls forget altogether about him because the vision of Jesus is the only abiding result. When people are attracted to Jesus Christ through you, see always that you stay on God all the time, and their hearts and affections will never stop at you. The enervation that has crippled many a church, many a Sunday School class and Bible class, is that the pastor or teacher has won people to himself, and the result when they leave is enervating sentimentality. The true man or woman of God never leaves that behind, every remembrance of them makes you want to serve God all the more. So beware of stealing the hearts of the people of God in your mind. If once you get the thought, "It is my winsome way of putting it, my presentation of the truth that attracts"—the only name for that is the ugly name of thief, stealing the hearts of the sheep of God who do not know why they stop at you. Keep the mind stayed on God, and I defy anyone's heart to stop at you, it will always go on to God. The peril comes when we forget that our duty is to present Jesus Christ and never get in the way in thought. The practical certainty that we are not in the way is that we can talk about ourselves; if we are in the way, self-consciousness keeps us from referring to ourselves. The Apostle Paul looked upon himself as an exhibition of what Jesus Christ could do, consequently he continually refers to himself—"And though I am the foremost of sinners, I obtained mercy, for the purpose of furnishing Christ Jesus with a supreme proof of His utter patience, a typical illustration of it for all who were to believe in Him and gain eternal life" (1 Timothy 1:15-17 Moffatt).

# XI. THE PHILOSOPHY OF THE PERFECT LIFE

*Matthew 19:16-22*

The occasion of a conversation is in many respects as important to consider as its subject. The occasion of this conversation was the coming to Jesus of a splendid, upright, young aristocrat who was consumed with a master passion to possess the life he saw Jesus possessed. He comes with a feeling that there is something he has not yet, in spite of his morality and integrity and his riches, something deeper, more far-reaching he can attain to, and he feels instinctively that this Jesus of Nazareth is the One Who can tell him how to possess it. It is to this type of man that Jesus presents a most powerful attraction.

## The Occasion of the Conversation of Perfection

### The "What" and "May" of Matthew 19:16

> *Good Master, what good thing shall I do, that I may have eternal life?*

Never confound eternal life with immortality. Eternal has reference to the quality of life, not to its duration. Eternal life is the life Jesus exhibited when He was here on earth, with neither time nor eternity in it, because it is the life of God Himself (see John 17:3). Jesus said, "Ye have not [this] life in yourselves" (RV). What life? The life He had. Men have moral life, physical life and intellectual life apart from Jesus Christ. This rich young ruler felt the fascination of the marvellous life Jesus lived and asked how he might become possessed of the same life. His question was not asked in a captious spirit. Watch the atmosphere of your mood when you ask certain questions. "Good Master, what good thing shall I *do,* that I may have eternal life?" The great lesson our Lord taught him was that it is not anything he must do, but a relationship he must be willing to get into that is necessary. Other teachers tell us we have to do something—"Consecrate here; do this, leave off that." Jesus Christ always brings us back to one thing—"Stand in right relationship to Me first, then the marvellous doing will be performed in you." It is a question of abandoning all the time, not of doing.

## The Obedience to the Conditions of Perfection

### The "Why" and "If" of Matthew 19:17-20

> *Why callest thou Me good? . . . If thou wilt enter into life . . .*

It looks at first as if Jesus was captious, as if the young man's question had put Him in a corner; but our Lord wishes him to understand what calling Him "good" and asking Him about "good things" meant—"If I am only a good man, there is no use coming to Me more than to anyone else; but if you mean that you are discerning Who I am," then comes the condition: "but if thou wilt enter into life, keep the commandments." The commonplace of the condition must have staggered this clean-living nobleman—"All these things have I kept from my youth up." The nobility of moral integrity and sterling natural virtue was lovely in the sight of Jesus because He saw in it a remnant of His Father's former handiwork.

In listening to some evangelical addresses the practical conclusion one is driven to is that we have to be great sinners before we can be saved; and the majority of men are not great sinners. This man was an upright, sterling, religious man; it would be absurd to talk to him about sin, he was not in the place where he could understand what it meant. There are hundreds of clean-living, upright men who are not convicted of sin, I mean sin in the light of the commandments Jesus mentioned. We need to revise the place we put conviction of sin in and the place the Spirit of God puts it in. There is no mention of sin in the apprehension of Saul of Tarsus, yet no one understood sin more fundamentally than the Apostle Paul. If we reverse God's order and refuse to put the recognition of Who Jesus is first, we present a lame type of Christianity which excludes for ever the kind of man represented by this rich young ruler. The most staggering thing about Jesus

Christ is that He makes human destiny depend not on goodness or badness, not on things done or not done, but on Who we say He is.

"What lack I yet?" Jesus then instantly presses another "if': "If thou wilt be perfect . . ." The second "if" is much more penetrating than the first. Entrance into life is through the recognition of Who Jesus is, i.e., all we mean by being born again of the Spirit—"If you would enter into life, that is the way." The second "if" is much more searching—"If thou wilt be perfect . . ."— "If you want to be perfect, perfect as I am, perfect as your Father in Heaven is"—then come the conditions. Do we really want to be perfect? Beware of mental quibbling over the word "perfect." Perfection does not mean the full maturity and consummation of a man's powers, but perfect fitness for doing the will of God (cf. Philippians 3:12-15). Supposing Jesus Christ can perfectly adjust me to God, put me so perfectly right that I shall be on the footing where I can do the will of God, do I really want Him to do it? Do I want God at all costs to make me perfect? A great deal depends on what is the real deep desire of our hearts. Can we say with Robert Murray M'cheyne— "Lord, make me as holy as Thou canst make a saved sinner"? Is that really the desire of our hearts? Our desires come to light always when we press this "if" of Jesus—"If thou wilt be perfect . . ."

## The Obliterating Concessions to Perfection

### The "Go" and "Come" of Matthew 19:21

> Go and sell that thou hast, . . . and come and follow Me.

After you have entered into life, come and fulfil the conditions of that life. We are so desperately wise, we continually make out that Jesus did not mean what He said and we spiritualise His meaning into thin air. In this case there is no getting out of what He meant—"If thou wilt be perfect, go and sell that thou hast, and give to the poor." The words mean a voluntary abandoning of property and riches, and a deliberate devoted attachment to Jesus

Christ. To you or me Jesus might not say that, but He would say something equivalent over anything we are depending upon. Never push an experience into a principle by which to guide other lives. To the rich young ruler Jesus said, "Loosen yourself from your property because that is the thing that is holding you." The principle is one of fundamental death to possessions while being obliged to use them. "Sell that thou hast . . ."—reduce yourself till nothing remains but your consciousness of yourself, and then cast that consciousness at the feet of Christ. That is the bedrock of intense spiritual Christianity. The moral integrity of this man made him see clearly what Jesus meant. A man who had been morally twisted would not have seen, but this man's mind was unwarped by moral damage and when Jesus brought him straight to the point, he saw it clearly.

"Go and sell that thou hast. . . ." "Do you mean to say that it is necessary for our soul's salvation to do that?" Our Lord is not talking about salvation, He is saying—"*If thou wilt be perfect . . .*" Do mark the *ifs* of Jesus. "If any man would be my disciple . . ." Remember, the conditions of discipleship are not the conditions for salvation. We are perfectly at liberty to say, "No, thank you, I am much obliged for being delivered from hell, very thankful to escape the abominations of sin, but when it comes to these conditions it is rather too much; I have my own interests in life, my own possessions."

## The Obstructing Counterpoise to Perfection

### The "When" and "Went" of Matthew 19:22

> But when the young man heard that saying, he went away sorrowful: for he had great possessions.

"Counterpoise" means an equally heavy weight in the other scale. We hear a thing, not when it is spoken, but when we are in a state to listen. Most of us have only ears to hear what we intend to agree with, but when the surgical operation of the Spirit of God has been performed on the inside and our perceiving powers are awakened to understand what we hear, then we get to the condition of this young man. When he heard what Jesus said he did not dispute it, he did not argue, he did not say, "I fail to perceive the subtlety of Your meaning"; he heard it, and he found he had too big an interest in the other scale and he drooped away from Jesus in sadness, not in rebellion.

Our Lord's statements seem so simple and gentle that we swallow them and say, "Yes, I accept Jesus as a Teacher," then His words seem to slip out of our minds; they have not, they have gone into the subconscious mind, and when we come across something in our circumstances, up comes one of those words and we hear it for the first time and it makes us reel with amazement. "He that hath ears to hear, let him hear." What have we ears for?

"Go and sell that thou hast, and give to the poor." Remember, Jesus did not claim any of the rich young ruler's possessions; He did not say, "Consecrate them to Me"; He did not say, "Sell that thou hast, and give it to My service"; He said, "Sell that thou hast, and give to the poor, and for you, you come and follow Me, and you shall have treasure in heaven." One of the most subtle errors is that God wants our possessions; they are not any use to Him. God does not want our possessions, He wants us.

In this incident our Lord reveals His profound antipathy to emotional excitement. The rich young man's powers were in unbewitched working order when Jesus called him to decide. Beware of the "seeking great things for yourself" idea—cold shivers down the back, visions of angels and visitations from God. "I can't decide in this plain, commonplace, ordinary evening as to whether I will serve Jesus or not." That is the only way Jesus Christ ever comes to us. He will never take us at a disadvantage, never terrify us out of our wits by some amazing manifestation of His power and then say "Follow Me." He wants us to decide when all our powers are in full working order, and He chooses the moment when the world, not Himself, is in the ascendant. If we chose Him when He was in the ascendant, in the time of religious emotion and excitement, we would leave Him when the moment of excitement passed, but if we choose Him with all our powers about us, the choice will abide.

"And come and follow Me." It is not only a question of "binding the sacrifice with cords to the horns of the altar," it is a rising in the might of the Holy Ghost, with your feet on the earth but your heart swelling with the love of heaven, conscious that at last you have reached the position to which you were aspiring. How long are some of us who ought to be princes and princesses for God going to be bound up in the show of things? We have asked in tears, "What lack I yet?" This is the road and no other—"Come and follow Me," "And thou shalt have treasure in heaven"—and on earth, what? "An hundredfold of all you left for My sake."

The devotion to Jesus Christ of our person is the effectual working of the evangelical doctrine of Christian perfection.

# XII. THE DISCIPLE AND THE LORD OF DESTINY

*Revelation 3*

## His Divine Integrity

> *These things saith He that is holy, He that is true .
> . . (Revelation 3:7)*

### (a) Harmony with God's Character

These words suggest that our Lord's unlimited sovereignty over human souls rests upon moral fitness. In Revelation 5 this aspect is again alluded to—"Who is worthy to open the book?" The appeal made to us by Jesus Christ is that He is worthy not only in the domain of God, but in the domain of man, consequently He "hath prevailed to open the book." The disciple's Lord is in absolute harmony with the highest man knows and with the highest God has revealed. The Bible is not the authority, the Church is not the authority, the Lord Jesus Christ alone is the Authority. The tendency is strong to make the statements of the Bible simpler than God makes them, the reason being that we will not recognise Jesus Christ as the Authority. It is only when we rely on the Holy Spirit and obey His leadership that the authority of Jesus Christ is recognised. The Holy Spirit will glorify Jesus only, consequently the interpretation of the Bible and of human life depends entirely on how we understand the character of Jesus Christ. If there is anything hidden from us as disciples to-day it is because we are not in a fit state to understand it. As soon as we become fit in spiritual character the thing is revealed, it is concealed at God's discretion until the life is developed sufficiently.

### (b) Holiness Supreme with Man

The disciple's Lord is the supreme Authority in every relationship of life the disciple is in or can be in. That is a very obvious point, but think what it means—it means recognising it as impertinent to say, "Oh, well, Jesus Christ does not know my circumstances; the principles involved in His teachings are altogether impracticable for me where I am." That thought never came from the Spirit of God, and it has to be gripped in a vice on the threshold of the mind and allowed no way. If as we obey God such a circumstance is possible where Jesus Christ's precepts and principles are impracticable, then He has misled us. The idea insinuates itself—"Oh, well, I can be justified from my present conduct because of—so and so." We are never justified as disciples in taking any line of action other than that indicated by the teaching of Our Lord and made possible for us by His Spirit. The providence of God fits us into various settings of life to see if we will be disciples in those relationships.

### (c) Highest Authority Conceivable

The highest authority conceivable for a man is that of a holy character. The holiest character is the Lord Jesus Christ, therefore His statements are never dogmas, they are declarations. In the Epistles we find the dogmas of belief stated and formulated; but Our Lord never taught dogma, He declared. There is no argument or discussion in what He says, it is not a question of the insight of a marvellous man, but a question of speaking with authority. "He taught them as one having authority" (Matthew 7:29). The disciple realises that Our Lord's statements never spring from a personal point of view; they reveal the eternal character of God as applied to the practical details of life.

## His Divine Imperialism

*He that hath the key of David . . . (Revelation 3:7)*

### (a) Abiding Sacredness of His Inheritance

The disciple's Lord has the key to every situation in heaven above or on earth beneath. Other powers that are not of Jesus Christ claim they can open the book, but the unmeasured blight of God rests on an intellectual curiosity that divorces itself from moral and spiritual worth. It is necessary to bear that in mind, for this is a day of intolerant inquisitiveness, people will not wait for the slow, steady, majestic way of the Son of God, they enter in by this door and that, and the consequence is moral, spiritual and physical insanity. All kinds of terrible and awful evils come through men having pressed open domains for themselves. They have refused to have the only authority there is, the authority of a moral, holy character. "But I fear," says Paul, "lest by any means . . . your minds should be corrupted from the simplicity that is in Christ."

### (b) Antagonists Scared by His Servants

The easy supremacy of the Lord Jesus Christ in and through the life of a disciple brings the blatant terror of the synagogue of Satan to bow at his feet. "Behold, I will make them of the synagogue of Satan . . . to come and worship before thy feet, and to know that I have loved thee" (Revelation 3:9). This is the age of humiliation for the saints, just as it was the age of humiliation for Our Lord when He was on earth; we cannot stand the humiliation unless we are His disciples, we want to get into the "show business," we want to be successful, to be recognised and known; we want to compromise and put things right and get to an understanding. Never! Stand true to Jesus Christ, "in nothing terrified by your adversaries." We find the features of the synagogue of Satan everywhere, but if the disciple will obey, all that power will crumble down as bluff by the marvellous authority of Jesus Christ. "Fear not, little flock; for it is your Father's good pleasure to give you the kingdom." When once fear is taken out, the world is humiliated at the feet of the humblest of saints, it can do nothing, it cannot touch the amazing supremacy that comes through the Divine imperialism of the saint's Lord and Master.

### (c) Alpha and Omega

"I am Alpha and Omega, the first and the last." Jesus Christ is the last word on God, on sin and death, on heaven and hell; the last word on every problem that human life has to face. If you are a disciple, be loyal to Him; that means you will have to choke off any number of things that might fritter you away from the one Centre. Beware of prejudices being put in place of the sovereignty of Jesus Christ, prejudices of doctrine, of conviction or experience. When we go on Jesus Christ's way, slowly and steadily we find He builds up spiritual and moral character along with intellectual discernment, these develop together; if we push one at the expense of the other, we shall get out of touch with God. If our intellectual curiosity pushes the barriers further than God has seen fit to open, our moral character will get out of hand and we shall have pain that God cannot bless, suffering from which He cannot protect us. "The way of transgressors is hard."

"I am the first and the last." Is Jesus Christ the first and the last of my personal creed, the first and last of all I look to and hope for? Frequently the discipline of discipleship has to be delayed until we learn that God's barriers are put there not by sovereign Deity only; they are put there by a God Whose will is absolutely holy and Who has told us plainly, "Not that way" (cf. Deuteronomy 29:29).

## His Divine Invincibility

> . . . He that openeth, and no man shutteth; and shutteth, and no man openeth. (Revelation 3:7)

### (a) Defied but Never Frustrated

The word "door" is used elsewhere in the New Testament for privileges and opportunities ("For a great door and effectual is opened unto me," 1 Corinthians 16:9); but here it means that Jesus Christ's sovereignty is effective everywhere; it is He Who opens the door and He Who shuts. "Behold, I have set before thee an open door, and no man can shut it." Behind the devil is God. God is never in a panic, nothing can be done that He is not absolute Master of, and no one in earth or heaven can shut a door He has opened, nor open a door He has shut. God alters the inevitable when we get in touch with Him. We discover the doors Our Lord opens by watching the things unsaved human nature reacts against. Everything Jesus Christ has done awakens a tremendous reaction against Him in those who are not His disciples—"I won't go that way." Insubordination is the characteristic of to-day. Men defy, but they cannot frustrate, and in the end they come to see that Jesus Christ's is the only way. The gospel gives access into privileges which no man can reach by any other way than the way Jesus Christ has appointed. Unsaved human nature resents this and tries to make out that Jesus Christ will bow in submissive weakness to the way it wants to go. The preaching of the gospel awakens an intense craving and an equally intense resentment. The door is opened wide by a God of holiness and love, and any and every man can enter in through that door, if he will. "I am the way." Jesus Christ is the exclusive Way to the Father.

### (b) Divine and for Ever "Never"

Some doors have been shut by God and they will never again be opened. God opens other doors, but we find these closed doors all through the history of man. Some people believe in an omnipotence with no character, they are shut up in a destiny of hopelessness; Jesus Christ can open the door of release and let them right out. There is no door that man or devil has closed but Jesus Christ can open it; but remember, there is the other side, the door He closes no man can open.

### (c) Desired Communion

In Revelation 3:20 the metaphor is changed—"Behold, *I* stand at the door, and knock. . . ." If it is true that no man can open the doors Jesus Christ has closed, it is also true that He never opens the door for His own incoming into the heart and life of a church or an individual. ". . . IF any man . . . open the door, I will come in to him." The experience into which Jesus Christ by His sovereignty can bring us is at-one-ment with God, a full-orbed, unworrying oneness with God.

# ABOUT CROSSREACH PUBLICATIONS

**CROSSREACH PUBLICATIONS**

Thank you for choosing <u>CrossReach Publications</u>.

*Hope. Inspiration. Trust.*

These three words sum up the philosophy of why CrossReach Publications exist. To create inspiration for the present thus inspiring hope for the future, through trusted authors from previous generations.

We are *non-denominational* and *non-sectarian.* We appreciate and respect what every part of the body brings to the table and believe everyone has the right to study and come to their own conclusions. We aim to help facilitate that end.

*We aspire to excellence.* If we have not met your standards please contact us and let us know. We want you to feel satisfied with your product. Something for everyone. We publish quality books both in presentation and content from a wide variety of authors who span various doctrinal positions and traditions, on a wide variety of Christian topics that will teach, encourage, challenge, inspire and equip.

*We're a family-based home-business.* A husband and wife team raising 8 kids. If you have any questions or comments about our publications email us at:

CrossReach@outlook.com

Don't forget you can follow us on <u>Facebook</u> and <u>Twitter</u>, (links are on the copyright page above) to keep up to date on our newest titles and deals.

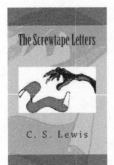

The Screwtape Letters
C. S. Lewis
$7.99
www.amazon.com/dp/1535260181

I have no intention of explaining how the correspondence which I now offer to the public fell into my hands.

There are two equal and opposite errors into which our race can fall about the devils. One is to disbelieve in their existence. The other is to believe, and to feel an excessive and unhealthy interest in them. They themselves are equally pleased by both errors and hail a materialist or a magician with the same delight. The sort of script which is used in this book can be very easily obtained by anyone who has once learned the knack; but ill-disposed or excitable people who might make a bad use of it shall not learn it from me.

Readers are advised to remember that the devil is a liar. Not everything that Screwtape says should be assumed to be true even from his own angle. I have made no attempt to identify any of the human beings mentioned in the letters; but I think it very unlikely that the portraits, say, of Fr. Spike or the patient's mother, are wholly just. There is wishful thinking in Hell as well as on Earth.

The Two Babylons
Alexander Hislop
$8.99
www.amazon.com/dp/1523282959

Fully Illustrated High Res. Images. Complete and Unabridged.

Expanded Seventh Edition. This is the first and only seventh edition available in a modern digital edition. Nothing is left out! New material not found in the first six editions!!! Available in eBook and paperback edition exclusively from CrossReach Publications.

"In his work on "The Two Babylons" Dr. Hislop has proven conclusively that all the idolatrous systems of the nations had their origin in what was founded by that mighty Rebel, the beginning of whose kingdom was Babel (Gen. 10:10)."—A. W. Pink, The Antichrist (1923)

There is this great difference between the works of men and the works of God, that the same minute and searching investigation, which displays the defects and imperfections of the one, brings out also the beauties of the other. If the most finely polished needle on which the art of man has been expended be

[1] Buy from CrossReach Publications for quality and price. We have a full selection of titles in print and eBook. All available on the Amazon and Createspace stores. You can see our full selection just by searching for CrossReach Publications in the search bar!

subjected to a microscope, many inequalities, much roughness and clumsiness, will be seen. But if the microscope be brought to bear on the flowers of the field, no such result appears. Instead of their beauty diminishing, new beauties and still more delicate, that have escaped the naked eye, are forthwith discovered; beauties that make us appreciate, in a way which otherwise we could have had little conception of, the full force of the Lord's saying, "Consider the lilies of the field, how they grow; they toil not, neither do they spin: and yet I say unto you, That even Solomon, in all his glory, was not arrayed like one of these." The same law appears also in comparing the Word of God and the most finished productions of men. There are spots and blemishes in the most admired productions of human genius. But the more the Scriptures are searched, the more minutely they are studied, the more their perfection appears; new beauties are brought into light every day; and the discoveries of science, the researches of the learned, and the labours of infidels, all alike conspire to illustrate the wonderful harmony of all the parts, and the Divine beauty that clothes the whole. If this be the case with Scripture in general, it is especially the case with prophetic Scripture. As every spoke in the wheel of Providence revolves, the prophetic symbols start into still more bold and beautiful relief. This is very strikingly the case with the prophetic language that forms the groundwork and corner-stone of the present work. There never has been any difficulty in the mind of any enlightened Protestant in identifying the woman "sitting on seven mountains," and having on her forehead the name written, "Mystery, Babylon the Great," with the Roman apostacy.

Out of the Silent Planet
C. S. Lewis
$7.92
www.amazon.com/dp/1536869929

OUT OF THE
SILENT PLANET
C. S. Lewis

The last drops of the thundershower had hardly ceased falling when the Pedestrian stuffed his map into his pocket, settled his pack more comfortably on his tired shoulders, and stepped out from the shelter of a large chestnut-tree into the middle of the road. A violent yellow sunset was pouring through a rift in the clouds to westward, but straight ahead over the hills the sky was the colour of dark slate. Every tree and blade of grass was dripping, and the road shone like a river. The Pedestrian wasted no time on the landscape but set out at once with the determined stride of a good walker who has lately realized that he will have to walk farther than he intended. That, indeed, was his situation. If he had chosen to look back, which he did not, he could have seen the spire of Much Nadderby, and, seeing it, might have uttered a malediction on the inhospitable little hotel which, though obviously empty, had refused him a bed. The place had changed hands since he last went for a walking-tour in these parts. The kindly old landlord on whom he had reckoned had been replaced by someone whom the barmaid referred to as 'the lady,' and the lady was apparently a British innkeeper of that orthodox school who regard guests as a nuisance. His only chance now was Sterk, on the far side of the hills, and a good six miles away. The map marked an inn at Sterk. The Pedestrian was too experienced to build any very sanguine hopes on this, but there seemed nothing else within range.

The Problem of Pain
C. S. Lewis
$6.99
www.amazon.com/dp/1535052120

When Mr. Ashley Sampson suggested to me the writing of this book, I asked leave to be allowed to write it anonymously, since, if I were to say what I really thought about pain, I should be forced to make statements of such apparent fortitude that they would become ridiculous if anyone knew who made them. Anonymity was rejected as inconsistent with the series; but Mr. Sampson pointed out that I could write a preface explaining that I did not live up to my own principles! This exhilarating programme I am now carrying out. Let me confess at once, in the words of good Walter Hilton, that throughout this book "I feel myself so far from true feeling of that I speak, that I can naught else but cry mercy and desire after it as I may". Yet for that very reason there is one criticism which cannot be brought against me. No one can say "He jests at scars who never felt a wound", for I have never for one moment been in a state of mind to which even the imagination of serious pain was less than intolerable. If any man is safe from the danger of under-estimating this adversary, I am that man. I must add, too, that the only purpose of the book is to solve the intellectual problem raised by suffering; for the far higher task of teaching fortitude and patience I was never fool enough to suppose myself qualified, nor have I anything to offer my readers except my conviction that when pain is to be borne, a little courage helps more than much knowledge, a little human sympathy more than much courage, and the least tincture of the love of God more than all.

The Person and Work of the Holy Spirit
R. A. Torey
$5.75
www.amazon.com/dp/1533030308

BEFORE one can correctly understand the work of the Holy Spirit, he must first of all know the Spirit Himself. A frequent source of error and fanaticism about the work of the Holy

Spirit is the attempt to study and understand His work without first of all coming to know Him as a Person.

It is of the highest importance from the standpoint of worship that we decide whether the Holy Spirit is a Divine Person, worthy to receive our adoration, our faith, our love, and our entire surrender to Himself, or whether it is simply an influence emanating from God or a power or an illumination that God imparts to us. If the Holy Spirit is a person, and a Divine Person, and we do not know Him as such, then we are robbing a Divine Being of the worship and the faith and the love and the surrender to Himself which are His due.

A Grief Observed
C. S. Lewis
$6.99
www.amazon.com/dp/1534898409

No one ever told me that grief felt so like fear. I am not afraid, but the sensation is like being afraid. The same fluttering in the stomach, the same restlessness, the yawning. I keep on swallowing. At other times it feels like being mildly drunk, or concussed. There is a sort of invisible blanket between the world and me. I find it hard to take in what anyone says. Or perhaps, hard to want to take it in. It is so uninteresting. Yet I want the others to be about me. I dread the moments when the house is empty. If only they would talk to one another and not to me.

CLAIMING OUR RIGHTS

Claiming Our Rights
E. W. Kenyon
$7.99
www.amazon.com/dp/1522757481

E. W. KENYON

There is no excuse for the spiritual weakness and poverty of the Family of God when the wealth of Grace and Love of our great Father with His power and wisdom are all at our disposal. We are not coming to the Father as a tramp coming to the door begging for food; we come as sons not only claiming our legal rights but claiming the natural rights of a child that is begotten in love. No one can hinder us or question our right of approach to our Father.

Satan has Legal Rights over the sinner that God cannot dispute or challenge. He can sell them as slaves; he owns them, body, soul and spirit. But the moment we are born again... receive Eternal Life, the nature of God,—his legal dominion ends.

Christ is the Legal Head of the New Creation, or Family of God, and all the Authority that was given Him, He has given us: (Matthew 28:18), "All authority in heaven," the seat of authority, and "on earth," the place of execution of authority. He is "head over all things," the highest authority in the Universe, for the benefit of the Church which is His body.

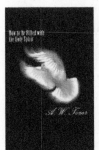

### How to Be Filled with the Holy Spirit
A. W. Tozer
$9.99
www.amazon.com/dp/1517462282

Before we deal with the question of how to be filled with the Holy Spirit, there are some matters which first have to be settled. As believers you have to get them out of the way, and right here is where the difficulty arises. I have been afraid that my listeners might have gotten the idea somewhere that I had a how-to-be-filled-with-the-Spirit-in-five-easy-lessons doctrine, which I could give you. If you can have any such vague ideas as that, I can only stand before you and say, "I am sorry"; because it isn't true; I can't give you such a course. There are some things, I say, that you have to get out of the way, settled.

### Home Geography for the Primary Grades
C. C. Long
$7.95
www.amazon.com/dp/1518780660

A popular homeschooling resource for many generations now. Geography may be divided into the geography of the home and the geography of the world at large. A knowledge of the home must be obtained by direct observation; of the rest of the world, through the imagination assisted by information. Ideas acquired by direct observation form a basis for imagining those things which are distant and unknown. The first work, then, in geographical instruction, is to study that small part of the earth's surface lying just at our doors. All around are illustrations of lake and river, upland and lowland, slope and valley. These forms must be actually observed by the pupil, mental pictures obtained, in order that he may be enabled to build up in his mind other mental pictures of similar unseen forms. The hill that he climbs each day may, by an appeal to his imagination, represent to him the lofty Andes or the Alps. From the meadow, or the bit of level land near the door, may be developed a notion of plain and prairie. The little stream that flows past the schoolhouse door, or even one formed by the sudden shower, may speak to him of the Mississippi, the Amazon, or the Rhine. Similarly, the idea of sea or ocean may be deduced from that of pond or lake. Thus, after the pupil has acquired elementary ideas by actual perception, the imagination can use them in constructing, on a larger scale, mental pictures of similar objects outside the bounds of his own experience and observation.

In His Steps
Charles M. Sheldon
$4.99
www.amazon.com/dp/1535086262

**IN HIS STEPS** The sermon story, In His Steps, or "What Would Jesus Do?" was first written in the winter of 1896, and read by the author, a chapter at a time, to his Sunday evening congregation in the Central Congregational Church, Topeka, Kansas. It was then printed as a serial in The Advance (Chicago), and its reception by the readers of that paper was such that the publishers of The Advance made arrangements for its appearance in book form. It was their desire, in which the author heartily joined, that the story might reach as many readers as possible, hence succeeding editions of paper-covered volumes at a price within the reach of nearly all readers.

The story has been warmly and thoughtfully welcomed by Endeavor societies, temperance organizations, and Y. M. C. A. 's. It is the earnest prayer of the author that the book may go its way with a great blessing to the churches for the quickening of Christian discipleship, and the hastening of the Master's kingdom on earth.

Charles M. Sheldon.
Topeka, Kansas,
November, 1897.

73572074R00062